Young Writers
2004 POETRY COMPETITION

ONCE UPON A RHYME

IMAGINATION FOR
A NEW GENERATION

Surrey

Edited by Steve Twelvetree

 Young**Writers**

First published in Great Britain in 2004 by:
Young Writers
Remus House
Coltsfoot Drive
Peterborough
PE2 9JX
Telephone: 01733 890066
Website: www.youngwriters.co.uk

SB ISBN 1 84460 434 9

Foreword

Young Writers was established in 1991 and has been passionately devoted to the promotion of reading and writing in children and young adults ever since. The quest continues today. Young Writers remains as committed to engendering the fostering of burgeoning poetic and literary talent as ever.

This year's Young Writers competition has proven as vibrant and dynamic as ever and we are delighted to present a showcase of the best poetry from across the UK. Each poem has been carefully selected from a wealth of *Once Upon A Rhyme* entries before ultimately being published in this, our twelfth primary school poetry series.

Once again, we have been supremely impressed by the overall high quality of the entries we have received. The imagination, energy and creativity which has gone into each young writer's entry made choosing the best poems a challenging and often difficult but ultimately hugely rewarding task - the general high standard of the work submitted amply vindicating this opportunity to bring their poetry to a larger appreciative audience.

We sincerely hope you are pleased with our final selection and that you will enjoy *Once Upon A Rhyme Surrey* for many years to come.

Contents

Bentley Primary School

Clewborough House School

Elmwood Junior School

Manorcroft School

Mytchett Primary School

Oliver Surey (10)	61
Edward Barrett (9)	62
Christopher Green (9)	62
Joel Pace (10)	63
Kayleigh Bennett (10)	63
Kathryn Roke (10)	64
Daniela Campitelli (10)	64
Srijit Venkat (11)	65
Emily Dowdell (10)	65
Natasha Ward (11)	66
Neil Gallop (9)	66
Dominic Machala (9)	67
Andrew Lockwood (10)	67
Thomas Fyvie (9)	68
Jack Lyons (9)	68
Ryan George (10)	68
Lucy Smith (9)	69
Rosanna Pinn (9)	69
Sam Kocher (9)	69
Jodie Stevens (10)	70
Francesca Reah (9)	70
Peter Hammond (9)	71
Abbie Parker (9)	71
Michael Lowman (10)	72
David Morgan (10)	72
Josh Kipping (11)	73
Alexander Barlow (11)	73
Charlotte Lindley (11)	74
Rebecca Holford (11)	75
Abbi Field (10)	76
Zoe Filshie (10)	76
Ryan Howson (10)	77
Nicola Gallop (11)	77
Laura Hylands (10)	78
Aaron William McDonald (10)	78
Dominique Quinlan (10)	79
Bromwyn Brett (10)	79
Max Dickinson (10)	80
Monique Lawrence (10)	80
John Hilton (11)	81
Ryan Wells (11)	81

Michael McKay (9)   81

New Lodge School
Melanie Louise Thorn (10)   82
Jonathan Eden (9)   82
Adam Giberson (9)   83
Matthew William Gill (9)   83
Joanne Tame (9)   84
Alexander Marshall (9)   84
Rebecca Erratt (10)   85
Anna Pahnke (8)   86
Stefan Pollak (11)   86
George Chellis (10)   87
Alexander Ward (8)   87
Max Ravenscroft (10)   88
Megan Hanlan (9)   89
Lucy Binns (10)   90
Chloe Buckland (8)   90
Harriet Barton (9)   91
Lily Akerman (8)   91
Matthew Eagers (10)   92
Alexander Heuvel (10)   93
Ryan Winter (9)   94
Greg van Staden (10)   95
Sophie Lee (9)   96
Christopher Ede (10)   97
Mackenzi Inouye   98
Ellis Clarke (9)   99
Camilla Froy (10)   100
Eddy Buckpitt (9)   100
Daisy Combridge (10)   101

Priory School
Bradley Fenn (7)   101
Naveen Kumar (10)   102
Stephen Rice (8)   102
Jem Wraith (8)   103
Jack Butt (7)   103
William Braterman (10)   104
Craig Short (7)   104
James Patston (11)   105

Edward Price (7)	105
Ryon Head (8)	106
Charlie Stebbings (9)	107
Joseph Stevens (8)	108
Jamie Budgett (8)	108
Francis Hudson (11)	109
Rhys Melville (8)	109
James Burke (11)	110
Jack Thoroughgood (8)	110
Jordan Lipman (9)	111
Matthew Clark (9)	111
Charles Stairs (11)	112
Peter Henley (9)	112
Ben Askew (8)	113
Christopher Bolton (9)	113
Rakesh Joshi (9)	114
Nirav Patel (11)	114
Daniel Herbert (10)	115
Daniel Westwood (10)	115
Arran Weeraratne (10)	116
Chris Beale (9)	116
Thomas Williams (9)	117
Henry Miller (9)	117
William Broad (10)	118
Priyam Patel (11)	119
Colin Russell (10)	120
Luke Mellor (8)	120
Joseph Hillyard (9)	121
Calum Stone (11)	121
John Whelton (10)	122
Chistopher Russell (9)	122
George Chesser (11)	123
Luke McCormack (11)	124
William Townsend (7)	125
Joshua Aarons (7)	125
Kemi Chaggar (10)	126
Jack Sayle (9)	127
Rocco Birri (8)	127
Jong Yoon Song (11)	128
Sultaz Ijaz (9)	129
Guy Mason (10)	129
So Okubo (10)	130

The Poems

Being A Refugee

Walking in the empty street
In my bare feet
Out of my country because of a war
I do not know what it's for
My heart is feeling petrified
I feel so terrified
Will my family die?
I begin to cry
My heart is burning like a flame
I hear God call out my name
My heart's beginning to sink
Like deep, black ink
Trying to find a home
But shivering like an ice cream cone
Police light up the way
Running from police every day
I roll up into a ball
Trying to get comfortable
I'm getting stinky and dirty
And I am feeling really thirsty.

Toni McPherson (8)
Ashburton Junior School

One Two Buckle My Shoe

(Based on the nursery rhyme 'One, Two, Buckle My Shoe')

One, two, buckle my saw,
Three, four, tick my door,
Five, six, make a cake,
Seven, eight, kick my gate,
Nine, ten, play again.

Charley Mackay (8)
Ashburton Junior School

Late Again

Oh my God!
It's ten o'clock,
I'm gonna be late again.
What if I have to stay in?
I don't wanna be late again.

I can just imagine
My teacher shouting again and again.
I've been late all week,
I don't wanna be late again.

On my way to school,
I know I'm really scared.
What are those kids doing?
They must be late as well.

I entered into the classroom,
I said that I was sorry,
But when I looked around,
The class was almost empty.
But I wasn't late again,
'Yippee, yippee, I'm not late again.'

Rhashida C Malcolm (9)
Ashburton Junior School

One Two Buckle My Shoe

(Based on the nursery rhyme, 'One, Two, Buckle My Shoe')

One, two, I need glue,
Three, four, I want more,
Five, six, show me some tricks,
Seven, eight, you're my mate,
Nine, ten, I have a hen.

Ben Fenton (8)
Ashburton Junior School

One Two Buckle My Shoe

(Based on the nursery rhyme 'One, Two, Buckle My Shoe')

One, two,
swim in
the canoe.

Three, four,
kick the
door.

Five, six,
mix, mix,
mix tricks.

Seven, eight,
television
fish bait.

Nine, ten,
hello, Ben
and Ken.

Jemma Morgan (9)
Ashburton Junior School

One Two Buckle My Shoe

(Based on the nursery rhyme, 'One, Two, Buckle My Shoe')

One, two, playing with you,
Three, four, eating more,
Five, six, eating a Twix,
Seven, eight, go through a gate,
Nine, ten, come back again.

Danny Masters (8)
Ashburton Junior School

Whatif

(Based on the poem 'Whatif' by Shel Silverstein)

'Last night while I lay thinking here
Some whatifs crawled into my ear
And pranced and partied all night long
And sang their same old whatif song.'

Whatif my brother turns into a vampire?
Whatif the school turns into flames?
Whatif my grandad trips over and breaks his arm?
Whatif the whole world turns to dust and fades away?
Whatif my grandma does not pay?
Whatif my mum and dad hate me?
Whatif I turn into a girl?

Everything seems swell until the night-time whatifs strike again.

Michael Sandiford (8)
Ashburton Junior School

Dionne

(Written in the style of Robin Klein)

Don't stay on the phone too long, Dionne!
Don't stick gum on the bunk bed, Dionne!
Stop playing PlayStation when you've got your homework
to do, Dionne!

(I sit here dreaming of the nice, cosy sea with my arms out free
having a good time, that's me.)

Did you tidy underneath your bed, Dionne?
Did you hoover the house, Dionne?
Did you finish reading that book, Dionne?

(It's really nice to see warm waves splashing in the sea.)

Sasha James (8)
Ashburton Junior School

Yasmin!

(Written in the style of Robin Klein)

Don't use my lipgloss, Yasmin!
Stop fiddling with Raquel's hair, Yasmin!
Turn off you brother's Game Boy Advance, Yasmin!

(I am trying on my new dress,
Making sure it isn't in a mess.)

Don't bite your nails, Yasmin!
Take your cousin's thumb out of her mouth!
Get out of that bath, you'll catch a cold, Yasmin!

(I am smelling the fresh water, and
I'm still your young, beautiful daughter.)

Yasmin Chanda Watson (8)
Ashburton Junior School

Janelle!

Don't bite your nails, Janelle!
Don't use my face scrub, Janelle!
Don't use my lipstick, Janelle!

(I am swimming, I am a mermaid, life is good being a mermaid.)

Clean your room, Janelle!
Put your coat on, Janelle!
I thought I told you to clean your shoes, Janelle!

(I am a fox running swiftly, dodging trees.
Another fox is chasing me,
But no one can catch me.)

Janelle Harris (8)
Ashburton Junior School

Whatif

(Based on the poem 'Whatif' by Shel Silverstein)

'Last night as I lay here,
Some whatifs crawled inside my ear.'

Whatif I forget to bring in my homework?
Whatif the bus is late?
Whatif my dad forgets to go to work?
Whatif I forget to go to school?
Whatif my house falls down?
Whatif my friend turns into a dog?
Whatif we have no school?
Whatif my teacher is not at school?
Whatif there is no IT suite?
Whatif I don't pass my task?

'Everything seems swell and then
The night-time whatifs strike again.'

Lauren Jennings (8)
Ashburton Junior School

Whatif

(Based on the poem 'Whatif' by Shel Silverstein)

Today while I lay there thinking,
Some whatifs marched in my ear
And pranced and drank all night
And sang that old whatif song.

Whatif I get expelled from school?
Whatif my friends think I'm a fool?
Whatif I do badly in my maths test?
Whatif in English I don't do my best?
Whatif my teachers think I'm asleep?
Whatif they think I'm making a peep?
Goodnight,
Sleep tight,
The whatifs said,
'I'm going to bed.'

Margaret Reid (9)
Ashburton Junior School

Whatif . . . ?

(Based on the poem 'Whatif' by Shel Silverstein)

I was lying in my bed and some whatifs came into my head.

Whatif I get told off?
Whatif I cough?
Whatif I fail my spelling test?
Whatif I don't try my best?
Whatif I don't eat my dinner?
Whatif I get thinner?
Whatif I have a baggy vest?
Whatif I turn into a pest?
Whatif I don't like school?
Whatif I turn all cool?
Whatif I fall on the floor?
Whatif I bash in the door?
Whatif I turn into a pig?
Whatif I grow a long wig?

Lee Chappell (9)
Ashburton Junior School

Whatif

(Based on the poem 'Whatif' by Shel Silverstein)

Whatif my gym teacher lowers me down?
Whatif there's a war in this town?
Whatif my mummy leaves me?
Or whatif I get stung by a bee?
Whatif I drown in South Norwood Pool?
Whatif I'm late tomorrow at school?
Whatif I fail my spelling test?
Whatif I don't try my best?
Whatif I get beaten up?
Whatif there's poison in my cup?
The whatifs have gone, they're out of my head,
The whatifs have gone, they're completely dead.

Tara Carosielli (9)
Ashburton Junior School

Whatif?

(Based on the poem 'Whatif' by Shel Silverstein)

Whatif Mr Casey makes us rhyme?
Whatif I do a dance that's not in time?
Whatif I don't do my best?
Whatif I have got a test?
Whatif I'm scared of a videotape?
Whatif I forget my school cape?
Whatif I can't sleep?
Whatif my mum makes me sweep?
Whatif I can't spell?
Whatif my sister makes me smell?
Whatif my dad is rich?
Whatif I look like a witch?
Whatif I don't like my chips?
Whatif I fall off a ship?
Whatif I have lots of money?
Whatif I don't have to worry?

Laura Dewsbury (8)
Ashburton Junior School

Whatif

(Based on the poem 'Whatif' by Shel Silverstein)

Whatif I don't like school?
Whatif I can't touch the bottom of the pool?

Whatif I look fat?
Whatif I turn into a cat?

Whatif I get rich?
Whatif I look like a witch?

Whatif I look like a chip?
Whatif I look like a cargo ship?

Whatif I look like my teacher?
Whatif I'm a football keeper?

Whatif I jump up and down?
Whatif I come to school in my dressing gown?

Jamie Whitlock (9)
Ashburton Junior School

Whatif

(Based on the poem 'Whatif' by Shel Silverstein)

Whatif I fail my spelling test?
Whatif I don't try my best?
Whatif my friends don't like me?
Whatif I bump into a tree?
Whatif my head grows bigger?
Whatif I was a digger?
Whatif I turn into a frog?
Whatif I look like a dog?
Whatif I can't walk?
Whatif I cant hold a fork?
Whatif I look like a chip?
Whatif I see a big ship?
Whatif I fall asleep in class?
Whatif I break some glass?
Whatif I can't tell the time?
Whatif I don't know how to rhyme?

Toyin Aofolaju (9)
Ashburton Junior School

What If?

(Based on the poem 'Whatif' by Shel Silverstein)

Whatif I forget my vest?
Whatif they see my hairy chest?
Whatif my trousers split and everyone sees my Barbie knickers?
Whatif I lose my brain? I'll be as stupid as a game.
Whatif I get the blame?
Whatif I win fame?
Whatif I become a dame?
Whatif I become a game?
Whatif I get the shame?
Whatif I'm not the best?
Whatif I become a guest?
Whatif I turn into a vest?

Gregory Searle Vian-Smith (8)
Ashburton Junior School

Whatif

(Based on the poem 'Whatif' by Shel Silverstein)

Whatif the sun won't shine?
Whatif the bed is not mine?
Whatif I have to go to school?
Whatif I go to swim in the pool?
Whatif I fail my spelling test?
Whatif my parents call me a pest?
Whatif I become fat?
Whatif I look like a cat?
Whatif I don't support Chelsea FC anymore?
Whatif I can't walk to the superstore?
Whatif I am sleeping on a football pitch?
Whatif I become a witch?
Whatif I hate chips?
Whatif they turn into cargo ships?
Whatif I don't live in England?
Whatif my parents take me to Finland?

Ben Davis (8)
Ashburton Junior School

A Refugee

I 'm scared,

A nxious,
M ad

A nd feeling down.

R eally
E xcited,
F eeling
U nhappy
G utted,
E xhausted.
E nemies.

Arinola Akande (9)
Ashburton Junior School

Whatif

(Based on the poem 'Whatif' by Shel Silverstein)

'Last night while I lay thinking here,
Some whatifs crawled inside my ear,
And pranced and partied all night long
And sang their same old whatif song.'

Whatif I get spots?
Whatif I get lots and lots?
Whatif my dog runs away?
Whatif I go to a café?
Whatif I don't go to school?
Whatif I don't go to the swimming pool?
Whatif I get 1 out of 10 in my spelling test?
Whatif I don't try my best?
Whatif I grow red hair?
Whatif I eat a red pear?
Whatif I don't know my name?
Whatif they think I'm playing a game?

Christopher Seed (8)
Ashburton Junior School

Whatif

(Based on the poem 'Whatif' by Shel Silverstein)

Last night I was lying in my bed,
And something came into my head.
It got me thinking and planning ahead.
Whatif I forget my vest?
Whatif they get a glimpse of my hairy chest?
Whatif I get hit with a brick?
Whatif if makes me sick?
Whatif I have to read a map?
Whatif I get a cat?
Whatif I have to go to Maday?
Whatif I don't get my pay-day?
I'm going to sleep at ten,
Before the whatif strikes again.

Nicole George (9)
Ashburton Junior School

Whatif

(Based on the poem 'Whatif' by Shel Silverstein)

'Last night while I lay thinking here,
Some whatifs crawled inside my ear,
And pranced and partied all night long,
And sang their same old whatif song.'

Whatif my cat gets sick and dies?
Whatif I wet my pants and start to cry?
Whatif if my friend talks to a stranger?
Whatif I am in real danger?
Whatif my nan goes all green?
Whatif my dad goes really mean?
Whatif the shadow in my room is scary?
Whatif I have a new granny called Aunty Mary?
Whatif my nan has a baby?
Whatif my hair gets cut off maybe?

'Everything seems swell, and then
The night-time whatifs strike again!'

Samantha Pyke (9)
Ashburton Junior School

What About If She . . . ?

Yesterday she gave me her teddy bear,
But she warned me, she said,
'Don't you dare break it!'

What about if she changed her mind?
What about if she slapped me?
What about if she hurt me?

What about if she kicked me
And I landed far, far away?
What about if she turned me into a witch?

What about if she killed me?
What about if she made me drink poison?
Argh! Phew! I woke up and it was just a dream.

Jessica Meta (9)
Ashburton Junior School

The Three Bears

Once there were three bears,
They all had their own chairs,
One was big, one was small,
One was going round kicking a ball.

Little bear said, 'Let's go for a run,'
'Sure, my little fellow, we'll have some fun.'
As they went to go outside,
A little thief came inside.

Amy was her name,
Then she went out and came again.
She tasted the porridge, 'Yuck,' she said,
Then she went upstairs to go to bed.

The bears came back and saw her there,
'Go outside because you're not a bear.'
Goldilocks fled down the stairs,
She went outside and said her prayers.

Aimee Kearney (8)
Ashburton Junior School

How Could I?

How could I grow blue hair?
How could I be the mayor?
How could I not wear a vest?
How could I be under arrest?
How could I pick my nose?
How could I work the hose?
How could I say 'Boo!'?
How could I go in the boys' loo
How could I sit down?
How could I go to town?
How could I pounce?
How could I measure an ounce?
How could I make my pencil ping?
How could I do all of those things?

Phillippa Scourfield (9)
Ashburton Junior School

A Refugee

R efugee
E xhausted
F eelings
U nwanted
G ripes
E nemies
E xception

T errified
R easons
A lone
V ery scared
E verything gone
L onely

C old
H eavy-hearted
A nxious
N ew Home
G utted
E verything different
S trangers

N ew country
E nemies
W et the bed

S ad
T errible
R efugee
A ching
N othing
G one
E nvy
R uthless.

Jacob Spargo
Ashburton Junior School

Goldilocks And The Three Bears

Once there was porridge on a table,
There, three bears lived in a stable,
There was Goldilocks waiting to pounce,
Before she did, the bears announced . . .

'Don't touch that, it's ours to eat,
If you do, you'll become dead meat!'
She screamed and screamed to the top of her lungs,
She opened her mouth wide and stuck out her tongue.

The tongue looked icky and slimy,
Although it looked well shiny,
There were lumps and bumps,
Baby Bear threw up in big humps.

Off the bears went, acting cool,
Goldilocks said, 'You fool.'
Goldilocks then drank the porridge,
She said, 'Wait a minute, don't I have college?'

Goldilocks went to bed,
The first bed was way too big for her little head,
The bears came back,
While she was still having a nap.

Who knows what happened to Goldilocks?
Maybe she received a great shock,
What if she had gone and died?
'I wish she had,' the bears cried!

David Hermanstein (9)
Ashburton Junior School

Golidlocks And The Three Bears

Once upon a time there were three bears,
Who loved to play tricky, funny dares.
Mum cooked some porridge,
Then they went for a walk through the road Corridge.
Golidlocks walked in the house,
And found a cute mouse.
The little girl ate the porridge,
'I hope Dad won't find out I'm not at college.'
I would love to sit down
And wear a golden crown.
I want to have a sleep,
Instead of counting sheep.'
The bears came home.
'Oh no, I need my comb.
What a fuss, it's my dad,
Oh no, now he knows I'm bad.'
Then Goldilocks had her cake,
That the bears did make.

Hannah Murray (8)
Ashburton Junior School

The Maths Test

I went to school today,
I forgot I had a test.
When my teacher gave me it,
I really tried my best.

My teacher said to me,
'I want to see your dad.'
I didn't want him to find out,
That I was very bad.

When I woke up the very next morning,
My dad came to say,
You weren't too bad,
You got a level A.

Jessica Potter (8)
Ashburton Junior School

Why?

Why do I have to go to school?
Why do I have to go to the pool?
Why do I have to get in the car?
Why does my dad go to the bar?
Why does my mum go to the shop?
Why do I always get caught by a cop?
Why do I have to eat a chip?
Why do I get a big whip?
Why does my sister eat baby food
Why does my brother act like a dude?
Why does my mum play the drum?
Why does my sister always say, 'Yum!'?
Why do I jump up and down?
Why do I wear a dressing gown?

Now all my 'Whys?' have gone away,
Now I can play all day.

Louisa Davies (8)
Ashburton Junior School

The School Play

The school play is coming near,
Whatever shall I do?
What if I have stage fright?
What if I need the loo?

The night before the day,
I really wanted to cry,
I told my mum I'd be good,
I knew I'd told a lie.

On the day I was really worried
Of course, I still hurried.
'Oh no, I'm on the stage!
And now I'm filled with rage.'

Maisie Wagland (8)
Ashburton Junior School

The Three Bears

Once there were three ugly bears,
Who each had different coloured hairs,
The oldest bear was really scary,
But the medium was just - hairy!
The smallest bear was very small,
Even though the others were tall.

One day, the mother made some food,
It was too hot, so they walked in the woods.
Goldilocks came and knocked on the door,
She fingered her hair, the colour of straw.
No one was in, she decided to
Go in, then wondered what to do.

She picked up her skirts and went into the house,
And across the floor, scurried a mouse.
She decided to climb up the stairs,
Whilst picking up some beary hairs.
She did so, and looked into the bedroom,
So messy, she thought, and picked up the broom.

Then she thought, *I've changed my mind
I don't think I'll be that kind.*
She put the broom back and climbed into bed,
'Stop throbbing!' she said angrily, to her head.
But back came the three scary bears,
Whilst Goldilocks was having nightmares.

They thudded up the creaking stairs,
(Goldilocks was still having nightmares!)
They went to where Goldilocks was sleeping,
Baby Bear had started weeping,
They towered over Goldilocks in her bed,
Bang! Bang! Bang! They shot her dead!

Rachel Chatterjee (8)
Ashburton Junior School

Goldilocks And The Three Bears

One time there was a family of bears,
At lunch they would say their prayers.
They went out for a little walk,
Mother said, 'Come, let's talk.'
But what they did not know,
There was a young girl, whose hair did glow,
Who walked to their door which was very low.
'Oh, shall I go in?'
Said the girl who had fair skin.
She walked through the door,
And slipped on the floor.
'Ow!' she said, 'I've messed my hair,'
And then she spotted a wooden chair.
There were three, big, medium and small,
She decided to sit on the biggest of all.
She said, 'Oh dear, it feels too spacious.'
She sat on the middle-sized one, 'Good gracious!'
She said, 'There's still some space.'
She sat on the small one, it broke, red went her face.
She decided to go to bed,
She got in the big bed and fell asleep,
She had a dream, it was very deep.
Then the bears came along,
Next the neighbours heard a bang.
The bears chucked Goldilocks out of the door,
She cried as she hit the floor.
She wouldn't be going back there again,
Just then it started to thunder and rain.

Amy Knight (9)
Ashburton Junior School

Whatif

(Based on the poem 'Whatif' by Shel Silverstein)

Last night when I was in bed
I kept on thinking in my head
Whatif I'm dumb in school?
Whatif I'm a fool?
Whatif I turn and faint?
Whatif I can't paint?
Whatif I lose my toe?
Whatif I mess up in the show?
Whatif I lose my hair?
Whatif in school I'm bare?
Whatif I get eaten up?
Whatif I turn into a cup?
Whatif I can't hold a fork?
Whatif I'm a dork?
Whatif somebody tells?
Whatif somebody smells?
Whatif I can't funk?
Whatif I turn into a skunk?
Whatif the sun doesn't shine?
Whatif I can't tell the time?
I wish I would go to sleep,
So the whatifs won't make a peep.

Joshua Biddle (9)
Ashburton Junior School

My Trip To Jamaica

On the way to Jamaica,
I saw the wife's baker.
He was nice and jolly,
With a daughter, Molly.

She was nice and kind,
But I should have looked behind.
What a mean, horrible girl,
That ring made of pearls.

She was a real show-off,
I knew it was a bad boff.
I went to my family with a sad face,
My sister was crying because of her shoelace.

It was nearly time to get off the aeroplane,
And, of course, I was holding a frame.
I never saw the mean girl,
The one with pearls.

When I got to Jamaica, it was like black tar,
My family and I were eating a chocolate bar.
I saw my old, wrinkled, grandma,
And my aunty. 'Ta-ta!'

Omique Maxine Williams (8)
Ashburton Junior School

Lovers By Candlelight

(For no one in particular)

Roses are red,
Violets, blue,
Gold is the colour
My heart shines for you.

Roses are red,
In vases of silver,
Candles glimmer in their waxy bed,
But my heart always shines for you.

Roses are red,
Violets, blue,
Love is the feeling,
I feel for you.

Violets are blue,
Like the sky,
Stars shine up high like my love for you,
Shine like the light of the candle.

Roses are red,
Violets, blue,
Touch me and
We'll dance,
Me and you.

Daisy Harvey (9)
Bentley Primary School

Mobile - Kenning

News-bringer
Tone-ringer

Text-sender
Problem-mender

Memory-maker
Picture-taker

Time-keeper
Message-seeker.

Oliver Jenner (10)
Bentley Primary School

Dictionary - Kenning

Page-turner
Silent-murmur
Eye-catcher
Adventure-hatcher
Hobby-taker
Story-maker
Knowledge-finder
Word-combiner
Spine-chiller
Library-filler . . .

Alice Rands (10)
Bentley Primary School

Car - Kenning

Cargo-holder
Horn-beeper

Road-creeper
Fuel-drinker

Motorway-user
Slow-mover

Brake-screecher
Wheel-squealer

Man-driver
Queue-maker

Fume-creator
Pollution-maker

Over-taker
Accident-maker.

Philip Armitage (10)
Bentley Primary School

Rugby Ball - Kenning

Bone-crunching
Teeth-battering

Ball-kicking
Scrum-making

Try-scoring
Conversion-taking

Drop-kicking
Points-earning.

Andrew Murphy (10)
Bentley Primary School

Parrot - Kenning

Tongue-screecher
Food-eater
Feather-flasher
Food-masher
Dozy-sleeper
Seed-heaper
Graceful-winger
Song-singer
Bar-climber
Perch-minder
Multi-colour
Good-mother
Sound-triller
Big-thriller.

Tom Dymond (10)
Bentley Primary School

Football - Kenning

Window-smasher
Head-crasher
Hand-feeler
Point-dealer
Goal-maker
Foot-shaker
Grass-tumbler
Finger-fumbler.

Jack White (10)
Bentley Primary School

Tiger - Kenning

Orange-striper
Growl-piper
Jungle-slinker
Fast-sprinter
Merciless-killer
Tummy-filler
Night-hunter
Proud-jumper
Graceful-pouncer
Cubs-bouncer
Cunning-peeper
Deep-sleeper.

Iona Cullen Stephenson (11)
Bentley Primary School

Burglar - Kenning

Lock-picker
Object-nicker
Door-breaker
Night-raker
Silent-creeper
Treasure-reaper
Sadness-maker
Jewellery-taker
Real-traitor.

William Fox (11)
Bentley Primary School

Dog - Kenning

Hair-dropper
Sofa-hogger
Loud-barker
Carpet-marker
Bone-licker
Flea-flicker
Stick-chewer
Grass-mower
Rabbit-chaser
Pheasant-racer
Mouth-drooler
Food-gobbler
Kiss-slobberer.

Lottie Milne (10)
Bentley Primary School

Eagle - Kenning

Wing-spreader
Talon-shredder
Graceful-swooper
Sky-looper
Beak-hooker
Fearless-hunter
Elegant-stunter
Animal-molester
Mountain-nester.

Emily Chissell (10)
Bentley Primary School

Snow

A blanket of snow covers Bentley.
Sparkling, white icing sugar decorates the cars,
Sprinkles the tips of the treetops.
Crystal daggers hanging from the rooftops look out below.
Cars like tortoises inching across the icy road.

Shivering horses stand in the freezing fields waiting for the thaw.
Gloved children stamp happy feet, hoping it lasts forever.
The snail trails of ice-shining car tracks,
And the dripping taps of icicles.
Freshly carved footprints made in the soft, crunchy snow.
Still.
Very peaceful and calm.

Mark Linegar & Jack Austin (10)
Bentley Primary School

Puppy - Kenning

Ground digger
Human licker
Bone flicker
Carpet ripper
Teddy tipper
Teeth like razors
Run like blazes
People lover
Food guzzler.

Will Sheppard (10)
Bentley Primary School

Bentley In The Snow

Glistening in the sunlight, creamy-white, crunching, crispy snow
blankets the ploughed fields.
Weary with the weight of whiteness,
gravestones bow like old withered men.
As the youngest crocus blooms,
the cornflower-blue sky looks over the horizon,
as the sun casts its shadows over the old battered gravestones.
A bark of a dog echoes from the distant hill,
smattering the air with a rattling winter breath.
The ghost of a wind passes through the haunted graveyard,
making the trees creak with an eerie squeal.
Icicles chatter and glint in the tinted, frosty sunlight.
Frostbitten ivy clambers up the weather-beaten carved,
peaceful tombs.
All that is left, *stillness!*

Beatrice Updegraff, Sam Panther (10) Ailsa Kiely (9),
& Barnabas Zubor
Bentley Primary School

Snow Over Bentley

Icing sugar snow settles on glossy bushes,
Its frosty glaze dazzles.

Car tracks glitter as the sun melts the dazzling snow,
Snow-laden branches bow low.
Freshly carved footsteps recover their original form,
Icicles drip and create iced puddles.

Gravestones have an inviting blanket of snow,
Grass shoots up looking for the spring sun.
Subtle snow melts as the temperature rises,
Snowmen on borrowed time, shiver as the night draws ever closer.

Sam Llanwarne & Thomas Goode (10)
Bentley Primary School

Rain - Kenning

Sun-blocker,
fun-stopper.

Flood-creator,
puddle-maker.

Drain-filler,
football-killer.

Umbrella-opener,
raincoat-soaker.

Wipers-faster,
misery-master.

Owen Dunne (10)
Bentley Primary School

Wales

Let the roving run
over hill and dale.
Deep pure-forested place
all beauty and grace.
Soft and gentle.
Anything is possible
in the hills and magic of the dragon's land.
Life is slow and safe
as time goes by unheard.
The slowness of the river
takes you downstream in such beauty.

Rosie Dymond (10)
Bentley Primary School

Bat - Kenning

Night-catcher
Lonely-hunter
Fast-flutterer
Sound-utterer
Sonic-pointer
Night-loiterer
Silent-descender
Moon-defender
Teeth-barer
Blood-sharer
World-turner
Day-loomer.

Max Dymond (10)
Bentley Primary School

Winter-White Bentley

Winter-white Bentley
Draped in snow
As the frosted icicles
Give off a glow,

The houses,
All covered in snow,
Stand bare and still,
While the cars
Drive very slow.

Ben Gillan (9), Oli Jenner & Will
Bentley Primary School

A Walk In The Snow

Icicles pointing like witches' fingers
Snow crunching beneath our feet
Footprints printed in the diamond snow
Delicate snowflakes pointing their toes
Gently settling in the trees
Calm snow
Subtle snow
A blanket of inviting snow covers rooftops
Wind whistling through chalk-white trees
Beautiful glass-shining icicles
The snail trails of ice-shining car tracks.

Megan Grace (9), James Brown (11) & Seb Wylie
Bentley Primary School

Hippo - Kenning

Mud-wallower
Plant-swallower
Ear-flicker
Baby-licker
Water-groaner
Loud-moaner
Mouth-yawner
Early-morner
Teeth-shower
Grass-mower
Tummy-flubber
Skin like rubber.

Laura Grimshaw (11)
Bentley Primary School

A Moonlit Walk

The moonlight was shining down on my back,
The sequins on my top glistened like stars,
He clasped my hand tight,
His fingers curled round mine,
The warmth was turning into sweat.
We walked down the pathway, our feet crunched on the gravel,
The river trickled past us,
The water shimmered in the dark.
We put our arms around each other,
He was breathing on me,
I felt warmth,
And then all I knew was that our lips were touching,
We were kissing.
The moon was going down,
And the night was turning into morning.

Bethany Burns (10)
Bentley Primary School

The Welsh Seaside

The cold water's tongue lapping around my frozen ankles,
Icy winds thrashing at the frothing, white horses,
The turrets of yesterday's sandcastles lying smashed into the
sticky sands,
Deserted beach, the odd forgotten bucket or spade, ownerless,
The twilight's breath blowing calmly around my bare shoulders,
Sand slipping through my wet and smattered toes,
The orange sun creeping under a cloud,
The pink sky turning to blue and the reddening sun changing into
a silver mountainous moon appearing
All is still.

Beatrice Updegraff (10)
Bentley Primary School

Girl Of My Dreams

Her eyes as green as ivy swaying in the breeze,
her smile as bright as fifty stars
and hair down to her knees.
Her lips as red as roses
and skin as soft as rain,
every night I dream of her
oh, when will I see her again?

She is deep within my soul
and locked inside my heart,
I think of her every day
and I wish we were never apart.

Jacob Heugh (9)
Bentley Primary School

Croc - Kenning

Jaw-snapper,
Tail-flapper.

Deer-eater,
Man-beater.

Tooth-gnasher,
Bone-smasher.

Fast-runner,
Fish stunner.

Joe Butler (11)
Bentley Primary School

Bentley In The Snow

Toe-tingling, crunchy crisp,
A blanket of snow covers Bentley.
Winds slicing with icy precision,
Gnawing viciously at beds of stone.

Sugary snow, icing the land, bringing us laughter and joy.

Deep green holly - breathtaking
As it catches precious glistening drops of snow,
Cradling the delicate flakes,
With its prickly edge and soft green centre.

Sugary snow, icing the land, bringing us laughter and joy.

The sun dazzles the silent snow,
Ancient tombs long-forgotten.
Bringing back curses and cruelty,
Myths and memories.

Sugary snow, icing the land, bringing us laughter and joy.

Snail trails following the winding country lanes,
But there are other tracks winding their way,
At the side of the road like a snake,
On a hunt for its prey.

Sugary snow, icing the land, bringing us laughter and joy.

A chandelier of glittering icicles decorate the graveyard,
Hiding from all its mysterious secrets.
The snow envelops,
Soon the fun is over,
As the snow rests to sleep.

G
  o
    n
      e.

Jess Wilson, Daisy Harvey & James Mealing (10)
Bentley Primary School

Caged Gorilla

Sitting in his cage day after day.
Thinking of the life he wants to be in.
A small caged box that's where he lives
And he knows that he can't escape.

The people are all around, never giving up.
Not seeing the point of life.
He's like an unblossomed flower
And every day he loses faith.

The food he's given is only pills.
Only some water that's not enough.
If he comes out, he knows what'll happen.
They try to be kind but they don't do much.

Always so cold, they don't really care.
He's a mighty, great animal but not much anymore.

Staring at the walls, they're as black as Hell's door!

Jonathan Gibbs (10)
Clewborough House School

Never Forget

I am a lion stuck in a cage
but I will never forget my old rage.
I used to run freely in the sun
but now I'm alone again.

I will never forget my freedom
because now I'm stuck in one cage.
People outside having fun
while I'm in here burning in the sun.

All I have is a dream of my old life,
the only time I had fun.
I will never forget that my life was bliss,
but now it's a horrid pain.
I will never ever forget how my life began.

Dennis McInnes (11)
Clewborough House School

The Polar Bear

What is the bear's temperature?
Is he hot?
Is he cold?
Who knows? It's a cruel world.

Does he want to perform tricks?
No! He does *not* want to jump through hoops.
Why? Does he have to do the tricks?
No, he doesn't!

He lies down:
But then he gets whipped
The polar bear gets up
And then he plays out tricks again.

Then the performance is finished
He tries to lie down but he's not allowed,
It's time for practise
The trainer hits so hard the polar bear collapses.
Why did he have to do that?
Who knows? It's a cruel world.

Adam Wicks (11)
Clewborough House School

The Insane Polar Bear

The insane polar bear
is fluffy and white
he comes out at night
when all the people have gone home.

He worries about what they think
and how could he be better.
He tries and tries, how he does it nobody knows
till someone shouts, 'Go on, do it again!'

Charlotte Sheehan (10)
Clewborough House School

The Homesick Gorilla

He remembers his homeland
Where he could roam free,
Protecting his family
And playing with glee.

He cannot sit down
As a result of the whip,
He can barely walk
Or tighten his grip.

He misses his friends
And climbing down vines,
Now all he hears
Are children's long whines.

He no longer roars
Because there is no point to do so,
He wants revenge on his hunter
For all the whip marks on his torso.

Back to his family,
Is where he wants to be,
He wants to be fed well
With fruit from the mango trees.

Callum Gerrish (10)
Clewborough House School

The Monkey With No Life

I came out of the darkness
but knew what I would find
a thousand eyes were staring
watching my teeth grind

I did some tricks on the ropes
I clambered down the slide
but all the while I knew
it was nothing like a ride

Then came the feeders
so I hid up in a tree
but they didn't care
anything about poor me

I came down from my perch
I sat on the grass
I knew it was stupid
I knew they'd only laugh

So here I am dreaming
about my life as a child
my one wish in my whole life
is just to run wild!

Robert Fail (10)
Clewborough House School

The Mighty Lion

The mighty lion stands, forgetting what it's like
to roar around in the dry, hot savannah.
Now stuck in a cage, he tries to roar,
yet only silence draws out of his huge mouth
lined with teeth as sharp as knives.

The mighty lion lies remembering the old summer days
lying on *real* rocks, not fibreglass mocks.
He tries to forget the enduring gaze of his mate,
as it brings him pain.

This mighty lion dwindles on the edge of life
as he sits and he waits for his last few breaths to come,
as he sits still, alone and glum.

He gazes at the strange visitors entering his cage,
he sits and waits as a truck drives closer
he is tranquillised and dragged into the truck.

As he wakes up, he sees a well-known face;
he remembers this lion and the sounds around.
He's back home in the savannah, a king once again!
He hopes that this will not happen to any of them.

Oscar Hyde (11)
Clewborough House School

Nothing Against The World

Dear Leopard, do you remember what it was like
When you sat up high in the golden sun?
When you played with your cubs and rolled in the grass?
How time went by.
With nothing against the world.

Then one day your joy came to an end.
Everything was still.
When that cage dropped how you roared with all your might
Trying to escape,
As they loaded you into the truck.
Your family and forest green disappeared.
With nothing against the world.

Every time you hear your cage open you sit and wish
That they're going to take you back to your family.
But it's the same old keepers that come.
At night when everyone has gone,
You go into your artificial cave and a tiny tear rolls from your eye.
You fall asleep thinking about your cubs.
With nothing against the world.

Now you sit in your cold and isolated cage.
You are starving and lonely,
With no one to protect you against the cruelty of captivity.
Only the hope of being reunited with your family
Gives you the will to survive.
With nothing against the world.

Zara Walker (10)
Clewborough House School

The Suffering Elephant

As I entered the big, blue tent,
All I heard was clapping.
I sat down at my seat,
While watching what was going on.

Then as I was watching,
A big, grey elephant came out.
Everyone was laughing,
But I was not.

His big, dull eyes told me that he was
Wanting to get out.
He was being beaten with a big, black bar,
Which left marks the size of an adult's wrists.

Just looking made me want to shout, *'Stop!'*
I looked down, the elephant had a big gash
Right on his foot.
I shudder to think what they do to him
When he's practising!

Anna Martin (11)
Clewborough House School

Wretched Cage

His eyes of flame are all but gone,
His claws are blunt because of age
His fur is black from lack of shade
His mind is shattered by a wretched cage.

He wants to run free from cages
Thinking of everything but his capture
But he's still inside dying from age
His mind is shattered by a wretched cage

He thinks of times when he could run around
Not of chains by which he's bound
He wishes the keepers would turn over a page
His mind is shattered by a wretched cage.

Matthew Smedley (10)
Clewborough House School

It's My Birthday

Loads of boys
Bought some toys
And started to make noise.

Mum had to bake
A beautiful cake
Which she had to make.

We decorated the rooms
With balloons
And we had some tunes.

After we ate food
Some girls were rude
And called me 'Dude'.

At the party
The boy, Marty,
Was really arty.

It is my birthday!

Arunothayan Suntharamoorthy (9)
Elmwood Junior School

My Cousin

I love my cousin
She is the best in the world
She is very kind.

She is fair to anyone
Even you as well
I love my cousin indeed.

Larome Hyde (8)
Elmwood Junior School

Summer Song

Summer comes
And summer goes
Summer is hot . . . summer sun
　　Summer sun
　　Summer sun
　　Summer sun
　　Summer sun.
Hot and dry
And dehydrating
Summer sun . . . summer fun
　　Summer fun
　　Summer fun
　　Summer fun
　　Summer fun.
Leaves on trees
Winds don't blow
Summer sun and fun
　　Summer sun and fun
　　Summer sun and fun
　　Summer sun and fun
　　Summer sun and fun.

David Lovejoy (9)
Elmwood Junior School

Summer

Summer is a spell of green.
When the sun comes up the petals open.
Up in the sky blackbirds fly.
The grass is soft, the tree trunks are rough.
Branches of the tree are tough.
Green leaves have grown on the old tree.
Children play while their hearts beat.

Kala Barathi (8)
Elmwood Junior School

My Birthday

It's Danielle's birthday today,
we're going to have a great party.

We're going to have lots of birthday cake
and lots of drink and food to eat.

It's my birthday,
it's Danielle's birthday,
I'm going to have a great birthday,
I'm going to have all my best friends
round my house in the afternoon.

I'm going to have a great time
at my party at my house.

Danielle Louise Mercer (8)
Elmwood Junior School

Fantasy Of The Year Poem

January is so cool and brilliant
February is fun
March is really nice.
April - 'Wow, it's Easter!'
May is absolutely cool
June, it's fabulous
July, it's a birthday month.
August, it's fantastic
September, it's autumn
October, 'Wow, it's my birthday!'
November, it's still autumn
December, 'Wow, it's Christmas already.'

Lucy Koser (9)
Elmwood Junior School

School Poem

School can be wild,
School can be great,
School is something we should appreciate.

You get wicked lessons,
You get boring lessons,
But they sometimes cheer you up.

Whether you're happy or sad,
You should still be glad,
Because some people have no school at all.

Shahnaz Simpson-Plummer (8)
Elmwood Junior School

My Birthday

Let's bake a cake
For Bianca's birthday.
Hurry up, for Heaven's sake.

There'll be lots of sweets
For Bianca's birthday,
And many, many treats
That we would love to eat.

There'll be dancing and singing
For Bianca's birthday,
And lots of games we will be playing.

Bianca Nelson (8)
Elmwood Junior School

Summer Song

Summer comes
And summer goes
Summer's dry . . . summer flow.
Summer flow
Summer flow
Summer flow
Summer flow
Flowers grow
Burning hot sun
Summer's hot . . . so much fun
So much fun
So much fun
So much fun
So much fun.

Ayisha Syed (8)
Elmwood Junior School

My Packed Lunchbox!

In my lunchbox I have
A chicken and salad sandwich
Two mini apple pies,
I assure you that none of these are lies.

I have two chocolate bars and a strawberry lollipop,
When I spill my yoghurt someone cleans up with a mop.
My lunchbox also has a packet of crisps
And a tortilla and tasty salsa dips.

Now I've told you what's in my packed lunchbox,
You can go because I'm so hungry I could eat an ox.

Yazmine Purchas (8)
Elmwood Junior School

Winter Poem

Winter casts a spell of white.
Icy leaves like silver snow.
Time for the leaves to fall on the icy ground.
Nice snow with breezy wind.
Everything is twinkly silver.
Icy ground with snowy balls.
Champions that win snowball fights.
Snowy leaves with shivering wind.
Snowy grass and icy roofs.

Measha Kimberly Layton (8)
Elmwood Junior School

The Troll

I never slept night or day
because I saw a troll coming my way.
We scared the troll off to his horse
but when we saw him again he had a bit more force.
My people and I were outnumbered from the coal
but at last a knight came and killed the troll.
And at the end we rolled him to his hole
and that was the end of the *big, fat troll!*

Nijiharan Karunaharan (9)
Elmwood Junior School

The Happy Seasons

In the blue sky of spring this is what the season brings.
All of the ladybirds looking around,
Come and see the honey the birds have found.
Look at the sun rising in the air,
Bears being attacked when it's not fair.
All the plants growing because it's springtime,
All the fruit there are like apples and limes.

Ephraim Haywood (7)
Elmwood Junior School

Kids

Some kids are funky,
Some kids can groove,
Some kids can dance,
Some can't even move!
Some kids like to learn,
Some kids like to play,
Some kids like to watch TV,
Some kids like to sleep all day!
Some kids like to jump around,
Some kids like to sing,
Some kids like to read,
Some kids like to discover things!

Shannon McGrath (9)
Elmwood Junior School

Riddle

In the dark sky
I see a red planet
Shining bright
Red rocks that I can see
With a powerful telescope
The planet is the nearest to us
Who knows what's there?
We are exploring, is there life on this planet
That's not very far?

Trena Vas (9)
Elmwood Junior School

Winter

Winter is a cold time.
Winter is a chilly time.
Winter is a snowy time.
Winter is a fun time.

Hannah Lovejoy (7)
Elmwood Junior School

Summer Song

Summer come
And summer go
Summer shine . . . summer glow
Summer glow
Summer glow
Summer glow
Summer glow

Hot heat
Starts to flow
Summer heat . . . summer glow
Summer glow
Summer glow
Summer glow
Summer glow.

Vynesh Pillai (8)
Elmwood Junior School

My Pet

My pet is my friend.
I love him lots.
He is all soft and furry.
His colour is brown and black.
He has big dark brown eyes.
He's my best friend.
He's my pet dog.

Tina Diallo-Jack (8)
Elmwood Junior School

Christmas Poem

C hristmas is a special day.
H olly is everywhere.
R eindeers flying up in the sky.
I cing on top of your Christmas cake.
S nowmen are made outside in the garden.
T earing presents at home and at school.
M erry Christmas is heard everywhere.
A snowdrop drops on your shoes.
S anta Claus is best of all.

P uddings are served everywhere.
O ften snow falls on your hats
E ating and drinking at Christmas party.
'M erry Christmas everyone!'

Prijanka Rathakrishnan (9)
Elmwood Junior School

Tigers

Tigers are vicious.
Tigers kill and hunt at night.
Tigers are the best.

I wish I had one.
I wish tigers were pets.
Tigers are huge.

Some tigers are now dead
Because people shot them.

I love tigers no matter what!

Dina Wahby (9)
Elmwood Junior School

An Alphabet Poem About Me

I'm an *adventurous* girl in an average world.
I'm a *bad* girl in a good world.
I'm a *curious* girl in a knowing world.
I'm a *dangerous* girl in a safe world.
I'm an *environment*-friendly girl in a world that needs to be saved.
I'm a *friendly* girl in a big bad world.
I'm a *great* girl in a good world.
I'm a *happy* girl in a not-so-happy world.
I'm an *intelligent* girl in an intelligent world.
I'm a *jolly* girl in a jolly world.
I'm a *kind* girl in a cruel world.
I'm a *loathsome* girl in a big wide world.
I'm a *mischievous* girl in an open world.
I'm a *naughty* girl in a goody-goody world.
I'm an *original* girl in an original world.
I'm a *private* girl in a private world.
I'm a *quiet* girl in a loud world.
I'm a *restless* girl in a tired world.
I'm a *strange* girl in an ordinary world.
I'm a *tall* girl in a big world.
I'm an *unwanted* girl in a big world.
I'm a 'I want-a-*voyage*' kind of girl in a not-a-voyage type of world.
I'm a *wilful* girl in a wilful world.
I'm a *xylophone* girl in a X-ray world.
I'm a *yippee* girl when something good happens in the world.
I'm a *zigzag* kind of girl in a swirly world.

Jazmin Pereira (8)
Elmwood Junior School

Haiku

We have good friendships
Families are what you need.
Be friends forever.

Sneja Shaji (9)
Elmwood Junior School

Winter Poem

Winter casts the spell of white
Which is chilly, wintry and cold.
Old people get cold but some people
Enjoy the snow by making snowmen.
Robins with red breasts come.
In wintertime ice is as slippery as a slimy snake
And people walk by and sometimes slip.

Niva Rajendran (7)
Elmwood Junior School

Ten Presidents

Ten presidents working by a mine,
One got lost, and then there were nine.

Nine presidents eating chocolate cake,
One ate too much, and then there were eight.

Eight presidents taking a trip to Devon,
One misread the map, and then there were seven.

Seven presidents playing dirty tricks,
One took it too seriously, and then there were six.

Six presidents working near a hive,
One got stung, and then there were five.

Five presidents buying a new door,
One got his fingers trapped, and then there were four.

Four presidents playing near the sea,
One nearly drowned, and then there were three.

Three presidents trying out something new,
One didn't like it, and then there were two.

Two presidents doing something fun,
One got bored and then there was one.

One president eating a chocolate bun,
He ate too quickly, and then there were none.

Melissa Snowden (10) & Rebecca Hindhaugh (11)
Manorcroft School

Feelings

I want to see sense,
I want to see future,
I want to see friends,
I want to see nature.

But why do I feel so lonely and sad?
I really wish I never had.

I really wish I'd said that word,
I really wish I saw that bird.

But why do I feel so happy and glad,
When I should be lonely and sad?

Now is the time to say goodbye,
I'll see you soon so please don't cry.

Jessica Donelan (9)
Manorcroft School

When You Are Lonely

When you're lonely
you feel sad
your friends don't like you.

You sit and stare
at your friends
they look so happy.

You are sad
on your own
daydreaming all the time.

The day is over
your friends have gone
you're on your own.

Ryan Holland (10)
Manorcroft School

My Teddy Bear

My teddy bear is ginger
He has lots of stitches,
His eyes are blue,
And he wears yellow breeches.

I sit him upright
At the end of my bed,
But by morning time
He's by my head.

I haven't quite figured out
Why this is,
But between you and me
I think it's this.

In the night when I'm asleep
He wakes up and starts to creep,
Up my duvet to my head
Then falls asleep upon my bed.

Jessica Vosloo (9)
Manorcroft School

We're Moving To Devon

We're moving to Devon
I heard on the phone
A place in Torrington
Will be my new home.

I don't want to leave
My school, teachers or friends
But I think every beginning
Has its own end.

But I guess living next door
To a friend would be cool
A playing field on one side
With a great, big, new school.

Alex Taversey-Veal (9)
Manorcroft School

Earth

The sun is bright,
The moon is calm.
The grass is green
On the farm.

The sheep go, 'Baa.'
The cows go, 'Moo.'
Guess what? We're
Animals too.

The colours are
Bright.
You can see them
At night.

The sky
Is beautiful at night,
The sky
Is beautiful when it's light

People are here
We live on this
Planet
We're called Mr or Miss.

Jessica Wall (10)
Manorcroft School

The Ocean

The waves crash
And the mermaids sing
The dolphins leap
And the fishes swim.
The ocean's big
The ocean's huge
The ocean's here
For me and you!

Francesca Dickens (8)
Manorcroft School

Friends

Friends are there when you are down
phone them up and they come round.
Through good and bad they stay true
friends will always be
there for you.

Friends are special, friends are good
friends will share their Christmas pud.
Friends are worth more than money
because you can't buy a friend
with your pocket money.

I can be a friend to you
you can be a friend to me.
We'll share anything, any time
as long as you're with
me!

Matthew Hopkins (9)
Manorcroft School

Friends

Do you have a best friend?
I did.
Did you tell her your secrets?
I did.
Did you laugh when she dropped her ice cream?
I did.
Did she say she hated you?
She did.
Did she play with different people?
She did.
The next day did you make up?
We did!

Chelsey Ludlow (9)
Manorcroft School

The Dreamcatcher

While every child is asleep,
Someone waits outside,
Who can it be?
They cannot see
For they have shut their eyes.

This person is from a far-off land,
You have something that's his,
He flies closer, closer, closer and
All that he needs is what you are thinking.
'I'll take it now,' he says.

'I want it,
I need it,
I want it now,
For you will not mind,
You're just a child.'

He pops out of the window,
He'll be back tomorrow,
Day is taking over night,
This person stays out of the shadows,
Stays out of sight.

So when you're complaining you can't get to sleep,
I'd just look out of the window,
It might make you think.

April Wells (10)
Manorcroft School

Snakes

S ilky, slithery snakes
N owhere to be seen
A little hiss you may hear
K ing Cobra could be near
E verywhere you put your feet
S nakes are waiting to defeat.

Joseph Watson (8)
Manorcroft School

The Sun

It shines so bright.
It's up so high you can't even touch it with a kite.
It's up in the sky,
So high, high, high.
It's kept us warm
Since we were born.
When it's not out,
There is no doubt.
The sun is so hot, do not worry,
It is much, much hotter than a curry.
The sun is much better
Than a big, big letter.

Jasmin Brown (8)
Manorcroft School

Pets

I have the best pet
you have ever met,
his name is Mr Clot,
he sleeps a lot,
he eats a lot,
he reads The Times,
he purrs in rhymes,
of this it is no lie,
only once he was seen to dance,
a sort of lively prance,
it was funny,
but made no money.

Chloe Steer (8)
Manorcroft School

Spooky, Spooky

Spooky, spooky,
spooky, spooky,
as the witches' brew.
Spooky, spooky,
spooky, spooky,
as the dragons flew.
Spooky, spooky,
spooky, spooky,
as the spider hangs.
Spooky, spooky,
spooky, spooky,
as vampires sucking blood with their fangs.
Spooky, spooky,
spooky, spooky,
as all the owls are hooting.
Spooky, spooky,
spooky, spooky,
as the skeletons are looting.
Spooky, spooky,
spooky, spooky,
as the ghosts prance.
Spooky, spooky,
spooky, spooky,
as the knights dance.

Lucy Langford (9)
Manorcroft School

Colour Change Chameleon

Turn red, turn blue,
Let's see what you can do,
Turn pink, turn green,
Try not to be seen,
Turn orange, turn black,
Don't forget to turn back,
Turn violet, turn yellow,
Choose a colour that's mellow.
Turn purple, turn white,
Stay out of sight!

Lauren Mullen & Louise Oram (11)
Manorcroft School

A Winter's Morning

I wake up in the morning still tired and sleepy,
I feel as cold as ice cream fresh from the freezer,
I look out of the frosty window,
And I see a soft blanket of snow,
The snow is falling like wet raindrops,
The snowflakes are as big as stones,
As I breathe in the cold air,
It tickles my tonsils and I laugh,
The birds have gone south,
Everyone is still asleep,
I am all alone.

Oliver Surey (10)
Mytchett Primary School

The Magic Box

(Based on 'Magic Box' by Kit Wright)

I will put in the box . . .
The sea as it sparkles like a diamond.
The cheering sound of a Chelsea player scoring a goal against
Man United.
The sound of a lion roaring.

I will put in the box . . .
The sound of a cheetah catching its prey.
The slither of a snake.
The sparkle of a glittering diamond.

I will put in the box . . .
The Queen's crown which is as golden as a gold medal.
The fresh smell of a scary, cold winter.
A blue bike which is as shiny as a crystal.

My box will be fashioned from shiny, glittering limestone
With sparkling blue and red spots and silver and gold in the middle.

Edward Barrett (9)
Mytchett Primary School

Vandalism

Vandalism, vandalism, it is bad
don't do it cos it makes you sad.
If you choke, it's because you smoke
don't flick your butts at the ducks.
Don't rob from us, it's not nice
you are scavengers just like mice.
Your graffiti, your vandalism
we've had enough.
You only do it cos you think you're tough.
Why do you do it? Why? Why? Why?

Christopher Green (9)
Mytchett Primary School

The Magic Box

(Based on 'Magic Box' by Kit Wright)

I will put in my box . . .
The water that sparkles like the stars,
And a ruby as red as a rose,
And an ice cube as cold as it is in space.

I will put in my box . . .
A roar from a tiger that sounds like the thunder,
And a diamond that sparkles like the sun on the shimmering sand,
The sound of the waves crashing on the rocks.

I will put in my box . . .
A snake slithering in the shimmering sand in the sparkling sunlight,
And athletes that run as fast as a cheetah,
And a lizard whose skin is as leathery as an elephant's skin,.

My box is fashioned from,
Pieces of the moon, stars and other planets that make it a
strong and sturdy box.

Joel Pace (10)
Mytchett Primary School

Winter Morning

I wake up and feel full of energy,
I open the curtains, all I can see is the sparkle of white.
The snow has settled and the morning has risen,
I hear nothing but the birds singing
And I see nothing but the snow glistening.
All is still. All is calm.

Kayleigh Bennett (10)
Mytchett Primary School

Fear

Fear is a dark, black, endless road,
A monster that haunts you each night,
A ball of fire heading for you,
Bringing you lots of fright.

Fear is like walls closing in on you,
Trying to kill you slowly,
It's like being in a small,
Dark box filled with screaming ghosts.

Fear is a ferocious animal,
Waiting to attack,
It's as fierce as a tornado,
That will never turn back.

Fear is following you all the time,
It's like an evil twin,
It will catch you when it's ready,
Don't let it win.

Kathryn Roke (10)
Mytchett Primary School

The Dolphin

Soaring through the water
What a really pretty sight
Leaping, jumping all day and night
It's as soft as velvet
And as smooth as silk
And if you touch it
You will feel a little chill.

Daniela Campitelli (10)
Mytchett Primary School

Death

Death seeks the bloody flesh of mortals.

He roams round the world giving no mercy to anyone.
He slashes victims with his magic scythe.
The scythe is as sharp as ten laser-cut diamonds.

As merciless as a cheetah chasing its rebellious prey.
Death is a roaring lion, waiting to come out and kill its prey.
The pain shoots through your spin demolishing everything in its path.
Giving you excruciating pain
That you can only have, once in your life.

It signals the end.
Agony reaches your brain,
Disabling your mind.
You start to hear voices in your head.
After this happens, the pain goes away and Death disappears.
He goes to 'mortal land' waiting for a fresh, new victim.

Watch out, you will die by his hand one day!

Srijit Venkat (11)
Mytchett Primary School

Rhyme Against Crime

Stop, stop in the name of the law!
Vandalism must go on no more
In a car, on a wall, graffiti is a broken rule.

Vandals, vandals everywhere
Go away, it's so unfair
You set alight to other people's stuff
Stop it now, we've had enough!

Emily Dowdell (10)
Mytchett Primary School

The Sun

The sun is a great ball of fire,
As hot as a scorching desert,
The sun is what makes stars glisten in the moonlight,
As sparkling as a cobweb covered in frost.

The sun is the master of the sky,
A queen ruling her country.
The sun is a ball that burns anyone who comes near,
As fierce as a tiger hunting for its prey.

The sun is a gas ball that stays up all night,
As tired as a cat being chased by a dog.
The sun is a forest captured by a flame,
As flaming as a spreading wild fire.

The sun is an enemy and a friend to other planets,
As friendly as a cat being cuddled.
The sun is an enemy to darkness
As sneaky as a fox stealing chickens.

Natasha Ward (11)
Mytchett Primary School

Anger

I felt like a volcano
About to erupt.
I was as furious as a fierce bear
On the rampage to get food.
If anything got in my way,
I would crush it.
I was really bad-tempered.
I put a thermometer in my mouth
And it went *pop!*

Neil Gallop (9)
Mytchett Primary School

The Magic Box

(Based on 'Magic Box' by Kit Wright)

I will put in my box . . .
A courageous knight who has fought with a mighty sword.
Two boats swiftly moving across the bright, sparkling water.
One rocket about to shoot off into space.

I will put in my box . . .
Two big pizzas that smell like lots of sweets.
A Chinese dragon blowing out scorching hot fire.
That feeling at night when I quivered and shivered
Like a snowman standing out in the snow.

My box will be fashioned metal
With a dragon breathing fire from the front of it.

Dominic Machala (9)
Mytchett Primary School

Happiness

I was streaking through the snow
Skiing all the way
I hadn't been skiing before
Down the mountain I tore

The wind was rushing through my hair
I saw a polar bear
It was a glorious sight
I went up a slope and took flight
The skiing was fun
The skiing was good
At the bottom of the mountain I stood.

Andrew Lockwood (10)
Mytchett Primary School

Happiness

I was so joyful
I felt like I wanted to scream
My legs were like jelly jumping on a bouncy castle
My brain was spinning round and round like a clock
I felt over the moon
There was my Game Boy Advance SP
As soon as I saw it I dived for it
I didn't put it down till dinner.

Thomas Fyvie (9)
Mytchett Primary School

My Dog Jake

My dog has gleaming eyes like a star in the sky,
He may have three legs but can still run,
He runs like a cheetah across the field,
He walks like a rabbit hopping everywhere,
He barks like a roaring lion,
His bite is as sharp as a jagged rock falling on your hand,
My dog Jake is the best dog ever.

Jack Lyons (9)
Mytchett Primary School

The Magic Box

(Based on 'Magic Box' by Kit Wright)

I will put in the box . . .
A shiny star that sparkles in the night sky.
A big castle with a crooked wall.
A snowman sliding down a hill on a snow sledge.
My box will be fashioned from gold with silver legs.

Ryan George (10)
Mytchett Primary School

Autumn

I see the leaves churning left and right.
The colour of the leaves is very bright.
That warm cooked breakfast is smelling right,
The one for me on such a cold night.
The birds are tweeting as loud as whistles.
The hedgehog hibernating under forest trees.
The rustling leaves are scrunching and crunching
In the cold breeze.

Lucy Smith (9)
Mytchett Primary School

Winter Morning

I woke up and I saw the dazzling white snow
While I was looking out of my window.
The snow looked as cold as ice on a winter's day.
The snow glistened like a pillow of glittering diamonds.
I can't believe that it is winter already
With the snow falling gently to the ground.

Rosanna Pinn (9)
Mytchett Primary School

Elephant

The elephant stomps along like a humongous earthquake.
His skin is as rough as concrete.
His ears are as flappy as a bird's wing.
The elephant's ear is like leather.
His colour is as grey as the clouds on a rainy day.
The elephant sounds like a well-tuned trumpet.

Sam Kocher (9)
Mytchett Primary School

The Magic Box

(Based on 'Magic Box' by Kit Wright)

I will put in the box. . .
A star that sparkles like a diamond.
The sand that shimmers in the sunlight.
The waves that wash against the shore.

I will put in the box . . .
The sound of a witch cackling over her cat.
The wind whistling and howling in the bushes.
The flowers opening in the light of the sun.

I will put in the box . . .
The trees with bright, green leaves like the grass in the summer.
The sound of the rain tapping on the window.
The birds flying high above the deep, blue sea.

My box is fashioned from gold, silver and blue wood
                              with secrets in the corners.

Jodie Stevens (10)
Mytchett Primary School

The Wonderful Parrot

Looking in the cage
What a beautiful sight!
A colourful parrot like fireworks at night.
It might be cheeky.
It might be rude.
It's just like a person, delicate too.
Its beak's like a lemon, cut right through.
Its feathers are yellow, orange and green, red and blue.
How lovely it is, such a beautiful bird.
In its cage trying to be heard.

Francesca Reah (9)
Mytchett Primary School

The Magic Box

(Based on 'Magic Box' by Kit Wright)

I will put in the box . . .
A unicorn's horn as sharp as a spear
A tooth from a dragon as long as a dagger
The sweet smell of home-made cakes.

I will put in the box . . .
A sting from the biggest scorpion
And a lonely, loud dog's bark that echoes
A lava-hot phoenix feather so another can be reborn

My box is fashioned from marble with diamonds
Inside is one big agate slice with tiger eye chunks
The lid is ruby and has a golden star on it.

Peter Hammond (9)
Mytchett Primary School

Summer Morning

I woke up to a surprise, the blazing sun shining straight
into my room.
The sun was glistening like a pillow of diamonds glittering
in the moonlight.
I felt like I was going to frazzle up because I was boiling hot.
I looked outside my window and everywhere I looked there were
flowers opening.
The flowers were as beautiful as an intricate mosaic.
It has finally come; summer is here to stay.
I feel sensational as the warm breeze blows on my face.

Abbie Parker (9)
Mytchett Primary School

Fear Is . . .

Fear is like a lion, it hunts and hunts
The colour of fear is a bloodthirsty red
It's like hunger, it can't get enough.

Fear is a cloak of death
It is as bad as a vulture's breath
It is as hurtful as ripping out your gut
It is as red as a baboon's butt

Fear is a poisonous stew
It always envelops you
You can't escape
It stalks you like a hawk
Fear is a monster, it feeds on your emotion
It makes you drown in despair's ocean.

Michael Lowman (10)
Mytchett Primary School

Boredom

I feel so fed up,
I am on a godforsaken planet.
Why can't I have fun?
I feel ignored
No one likes me.
I hate myself
I feel intimidated.
I watch the hands of the clock go round
Like some eyes moving
Left and right.

David Morgan (10)
Mytchett Primary School

Fear Is Like . . .

Going into a dark room and seeing a weird green figure.

Getting trapped in a room full of mirrors, seeing the
Grim Reaper's scythe.

Fear is a death cloak following you, trying to envelop you
while boiling in witches' stew.

Fear is like having a tonne tied to your leg, dropping
to the deep depths of the ocean, while being in an explosion
when scientists are making potions.

Fear is like falling into a black hole that is as cold as staying
at the North Pole for forty days and forty nights.

Josh Kipping (11)
Mytchett Primary School

Sea

The sea is an enormous sheet,
Spread over most of the Earth's surface
When it's rough, like a raging lion,
Gnashing any ship in sight.

The sea's enemy is a lighthouse,
Glaring over its rough waves,
Guarding any ship in sight,
Pulling them out of its shredding waves

When it's calm, it's a children's playground
Letting them all splash around
Swimmers racing back and forth
Trying to complete an obstacle course.

Alexander Barlow (11)
Mytchett Primary School

Seasons

Winter

Winter is wet and cold,
It snows as the days get old,
Playing in the snow, people having fun,
Not even playing in the sun,
Wind is howling all day long,
Everything is going wrong,
Rain is beating down on roofs,
Horses are banging their hooves.

Spring

Spring is a quiet time of year,
Not many people are here,
All the colours, yellow, green and white,
Are lovely to look at because of the sight,
The weather is excellent or bad,
Sometimes it might even make you sad,
Spring makes the days grow longer,
Some people might even become stronger.

Summer

Summer is my best time,
Trees are good to climb,
It is the hottest time of year,
Everyone I know is here,
You're so hot you will crisp,
Summer is fun, summer is cool,
It is hot enough, you can have a dip in the pool,
A good time to play,
You can have fun all day.

Autumn

Autumn leaves are falling down,
Twisting, twirling to the ground,
Autumn is a time when with leaves you play,
So come on out and play, play, play,
Leaves are drops of gold,
The days are getting shorter and cold,
Water in a field is like corn,
In the early morn.

Charlotte Lindley (11)
Mytchett Primary School

Darkness

Darkness is a scary monster,
Sounding like someone screaming,
Evil danger all around you,
Quick, quick, find help!

Dark is like a big, black cave,
Biting the gloomy air,
A monster scurrying to find animals,
Dangerous as the tide washing you away.

Darkness is a secret,
Hidden in the moonlit sky,
Black and white, lots of fright,
Damp and cold as an unknown place.

Darkness is a cosy bed,
Wrapped up warm in a duvet,
Dark when you are sleeping,
It's my favourite place at night.

Rebecca Holford (11)
Mytchett Primary School

The Seasons

Spring is like a field of flowers
Smelling as sweet as sugar.
The field is colourful
Like the rainbow.

In summer the end of school comes
It's like being let out of prison for six weeks
It's as hot as the golden sun
Scorching the sand on a sandy beach.

Autumn is when the leaves are coloured
It's like standing on bags of crisps
Rain plunging like a waterfall
Tipping to the ground in buckets.

Winter brings the fluffy snow
As white as cows' milk
The dewy grass outside
Delivers cold inside.

Abbi Field (10)
Mytchett Primary School

A Cheetah

Sprints as fast as gushing wind,
Eats rapidly like a starving falcon,
Its tail as smooth as a baby,
Sleeps as peacefully as a resting kitten,
As skinny as a Siamese cat,
Sweeter than a puppy playing,
Teeth as sharp as a great white shark,
Ripping its prey to slices,
Sunshine makes its fur glow,
Like a gold necklace catching light.

Zoe Filshie (10)
Mytchett Primary School

Fear Is . . .

As scary as giant murderers with poison knives,
As dark as when the sun goes out,
Greasy, infested blood dripping from the ceiling,
The murderer, prowling up the half-eaten stairs,

As frightening as being caught by bloodthirsty creatures,
As cold as a frozen Earth,
Death angels shooting Black Death at you,
Rampaging beasts roaming the world,

As heart-racing as a paranormal force
As shivery as a frozen bolt shooting up your spine
As life-threatening as walls closing in

Fear is death . . .

Ryan Howson (10)
Mytchett Primary School

Time

Time is all around us,
Time makes our day.
It follows us wherever we go,
And it makes your age.

You're young then old,
Strong as gravity and weak as a feather.
Times you have fun,
Times you don't.

Time is as slow as a tortoise trotting along the path,
It passes us every day and night.
Time has been around since the world began,
And time is your life!

Nicola Gallop (11)
Mytchett Primary School

Horses

Gently grazing in the fields,
Like a powerful vacuum.
Hooves of diamond pounding grass,
Horses canter, eat and roll.

Coloured black, grey, albino
Piebald, skewbald, palomino.
United, pony and horse,
Owners of the greatest force.

Flowing both mane and tail,
Like a wild, rushing brook.
With flexible, supple backs,
And their coats of velvet silk.

Laura Hylands (10)
Mytchett Primary School

Fear

Fear is a beast
As evil as the Devil himself

Fangs like a vampire

It is the emperor of evil

Claws the size of oars
It's there to stay, don't get in its way
As scared as a scream on a dark night
When your stomach squeezes tightly
Makes your bones shiver like an iceberg
Fear is a monstrous beast!

Aaron William McDonald (10)
Mytchett Primary School

Cold

Cold is a lonely man,
Miserable as grey clouds pouring with rain.
His ice-sharp teeth bite,
Slipping and sliding on his way.

Winter is hungry for light.
Is light late and dark early?
The light is a shy man,
Afraid to come out of the darkness.

The leaves are frozen fingers,
Falling to the ground.
The grass is a carpet of diamonds,
While it sparkles in the sun.

Dominique Quinlan (10)
Mytchett Primary School

Summer

Summer is an excited child going on holiday, happy and having fun.
Summer is an ice cream melting in the hot, baking sun.
Summer is the colour yellow, yellow like the sun, the sky is as blue
as the ocean, the grass is as dry and brown as a desert.

Summer means shorts and T-shirts.
Winter clothes packed away.
Theme parks are open so you can have some fun.
As you go down the waterslide, it's like going down a waterfall
as fast as a tiger chasing its prey.

Bromwyn Brett (10)
Mytchett Primary School

Fear

Fear, a snake ready to assault
Fear is spikes raining down on you
The pain rockets up your spine disabling your brain
Fear is so horrid it's like being shot with a gun.

Fear is a deadly spider about to bite
It's like a whirlwind ripping up trees
Like being stung by a hundred bees
A spaceship trying to abduct you.

Fear is a fire blazing around you,
Do not try to hide because it will tear you apart
As scary as death about to take a soul
Fear is a monster lurking in the shadows.

Max Dickinson (10)
Mytchett Primary School

Flowers

Flowers are as special as a new bundle of joy.
Flowers are as beautiful as a bride in her wedding dress.
Flowers are as scented as a forest of exotic plants
smelling like bubblegum ice cream.
Flowers are different sizes, either as big as a giant
or as small as a dwarf.

Flowers are a carpet, multicoloured, beneath your feet.
Flowers are a fast-moving car, whizzing round and round.
Sunflowers are the sun and the beams are the colourful petals.
Flowers are hungry children waiting to be fed.

Monique Lawrence (10)
Mytchett Primary School

Chocolate

As precious as the Queen's rings.
As sticky as old gum.
As crunchy as the crispiest leaf.
Softer than silk.

As white as a sheet of snow.
Dark as the deepest sea.
As milky as the surface of the moon.
As creamy as milk from a cow.

John Hilton (11)
Mytchett Primary School

Concorde

It is as fast as the speed of light,
It is as smooth as a snake's skin,
And is as airborne as an eagle.

The colour is as white as snow just seconds from the sky,
It looks like an arrow through the sky,
It is as tough as a tank,
And is as shiny as a brand new polished car.

Ryan Wells (11)
Mytchett Primary School

Rhyme Against Crime

This is a rhyme against crime . . .
Vandals, vandals, don't write on the wall
Vandals, vandals, you're not cool
Vandals, vandals, don't get that can
Vandals, vandals, we'll take you away in a van.
Vandals, vandals, you are bad
Vandals, vandals, you make us sad.

Michael McKay (9)
Mytchett Primary School

Overrun With Monkeys

The house was silent, dark at peace,
No movement outside, all noise had ceased.
When suddenly there was a screech,
And another, and another,
Until there was a dark shadow
Gliding down the stairs,
Very slowly.
I turned on the light switch
And there was a fierce, growling
Monkey staring at me.
He had fangs,
Black fur,
And blood dripping out of his mouth.
Suddenly I was overrun with monkeys,
Loping, leaping, lurching towards me.
I screamed,
And ran.
They followed me round the dark house.
Then it grew light,
And they disappeared,
And turned into dust.

Melanie Louise Thorn (10)
New Lodge School

My Dogs

Dexter the dog is nearly blind
He always seems to want to whine
He has a runny nose
And smelly toes
He has doggy friends and doggy foes.

Oliver, on the other hand, is small
He's Dexter's brother and comes when you call
If I don't like my tea
He eats it for me
And he loves to play tug and chase after a ball.

Jonathan Eden (9)
New Lodge School

Overrun With Cats!

Cats here, cats there
On the bed and in the chair
They bite the mice, they eat the mail,
They beat the dog with their own tail

The cats are purry and the cats are furry
They climb up the curtains and tear with their claws
They scratch the paint on all of the doors

In the garden they dig deep holes
Looking for insects and eating up moles
They have a bad habit of chasing the rabbit
And scaring him half to death.
Round and round the rabbit he runs until he is puffing for breath.

Cats here, cats there
Cats, cats everywhere!

Adam Giberson (9)
New Lodge School

The Storm Monster

When the storm monster *bellows*
Tornadoes twirl in the wind
Houses smashed to crumbs
And power lines fall over.

When the storm monster *cries*
Blizzards of rain form puddles
And children splash about
As they test their taste with their tongues

When the storm monster *sleeps*
All the clouds disappear in its mouth
The rain evaporates in the warm air
And children laugh and enjoy the clear blue sky.

Matthew William Gill (9)
New Lodge School

Emily The Tortoiseshell

Emily is my cat
My very own cat

She creeps around in the night
Waiting for that special sight

She likes to catch a bird or mouse
But dare not bring them in the house!

So on the doorstep she will leave
A present for me, I believe

She likes to sleep with me in bed
And likes to lie across my head

This is uncomfortable and so
Out in the garden she must go

I go and look for her in the morning
She jumps on me without any warning

Emily is my cat
My very own cat.

Joanne Tame (9)
New Lodge School

The Weather Monster

When the weather monster cries,
The roads flood as deep as oceans,
Children dash outside with umbrellas,
Splashing and splashing in the muddy puddles.

When the weather monster blows,
The trees fall and bushes rattle,
People grasp the swaying trees.
Chimney pots fall with a crash.

When the weather monster stamps,
Roads crack and people get swallowed up.
Houses crumble, children flee,
And swimming centres explode and flood the roads.

Alexander Marshall (9)
New Lodge School

Overrun With Ducks

The house was silent, dark, at peace,
No movement outside, all noise had ceased.
When suddenly . . .

An army of ducks came shooting out of a pond,
White ducks, black ducks, green ducks,
Fat ducks, flat ducks, bulgy ducks,
All the ducks you could imagine.

They flew down people's chimneys,
It made them very cross,
For the ducks liked being the boss.

They went on the sofas,
And even the chairs,
Some just stood on carpets,
And some went up the stairs.

They threw out everyone
Which wasn't very nice,
They made bread and butter pudding,
And even chased the mice.

So the crowds found themselves
Lying in the middle of the pond,
They chased everyone out,
But not James Bond.

He was locked up
In a chamber below,
By the ducks,
Who were very low.

This is what happened
50 years ago,
And if you don't believe me,
I'll take you there to show!

Rebecca Erratt (10)
New Lodge School

Animals Everywhere

In the jungle or the mountains,
In the field and in the house,
In the desert or the forest
You can be sure to find a mouse.

Find a barn with dusty walls,
Where horses crunch and munch,
Everything creeps and crawls,
While cows eat their lunch.

Look for a tree,
And you will see
Birds humming and singing
And owls hooting.

In a pond, near the forest,
You will find something jumpy
Being green called Boris
Who is a frog, very lumpy.

Anna Pahnke (8)
New Lodge School

Overrun With Snakes

The house was silent, dark, at peace
No movement outside, all noise had ceased
When suddenly, from a hole in the skirting,
Came a hissing sound.
Then an army of slithering snakes was all around.
They came in pairs, went up the stairs
And slid over chairs.
There were swift-moving sea snakes in the hall
And green grass snakes up the wall.
Scaly boa constrictors and adders on ladders,
Forced the rattlesnakes to get madder and madder.
Long graceful pythons came in from the cold.
They overran the house so it had to be sold.

Stefan Pollak (11)
New Lodge School

Overrun With Tarantulas

In my house, when all was quiet and at peace
When all movement had ceased . . . the tarantulas came out!
They were lean and brawny
Tangled and scrawny
All over me
But I couldn't see
They were black and hairy
Frightening and scary
As they crawled up my bed
They clambered over my head
They were rustling and bustling to get to me first
If I hadn't moved then I'd have been cursed
So I ran out the door, I was safe at last
And I slammed the door - fast!
Clawing at the door, trying to break free
I knew that they couldn't get me
But I just smiled
I was safe.

George Chellis (10)
New Lodge School

Sharkey The Shark

I have a pet called Sharkey the shark,
He's so strong he could sink an ark.

He swims about at the speed of light,
He never stops to rest for the night.

The other fish all keep away,
Because they are too scared to play.

He really is a super fish,
You'll never find him on a dish!

Alexander Ward (8)
New Lodge School

Overrun By Insects!

It was peaceful and quiet
Inside a house,
Nothing was stirring, not even a mouse,
And suddenly awoke a huge *riot!*
There were *insects* everywhere -
In the bath
On the chairs!
Woodlice on the fireplace,
Spiders biting Granny's face!
They marched through the neighbourhood,
Infecting all the neighbours' food!
Crawling through the tiny holes,
They ran through tunnels made by moles,
Until they reached the churchyard gates.
Those rotten pests were doing great.
But just outside the vicar's door
The vicar's wife shouted, 'No more!
I'm going to phone Angus McGhee.
He'll kill them all, for one small fee!'
And before the clock struck half-past four
He'd killed ten thousand, maybe more!
His 'secret' purple chemical spray
Seemed to make them run away
And by the time I'd done my chores
There were no bugs on the grimy floors,
And now our town is spotless.

Max Ravenscroft (10)
New Lodge School

Seasons' Tea Party

First to arrive at the party is Spring
Secondly in bursts Summer
Joyfully arrives Autumn
But last of all comes Winter.

Spring is wearing lamb's wool
Summer's wearing sunshine
Autumn's sporting orange tights
Winter's dressed in wrapping paper

Spring is having fairy cakes
Summer's sipping tea
Autumn's gobbling gateaux
Winter's freezing me

Winter departs with a whistling breeze
Autumn goes with a falling of leaves
Summer blasts off leaving a trail of sunlight
Spring leaves the hall shining bright

Winter trudges back to his white-carpeted house
Autumn rustles back to her leafy bed
Summer skips back to her snug little home
Spring lies down to rest her head.

Megan Hanlan (9)
New Lodge School

The Grasshopper

I pounce from leaf to leaf,
Making sure where I land,
To stop me from landing on a batch of flies,
Or making a move on the leader himself,
Which would be bad because you would be put on the shelf!
Forgotten and left to die alone,
From a world of happiness, just thrown.
But I'm a happy soul,
And don't want to talk,
About you know what,
So let's move on . . .
To a brandy shot,
To celebrate the remembrance,
Of my fiftieth birthday,
Which was in May,
A very good birthday, indeed it was,
When bees sang of money,
And sweet runny honey
Which nobody will ever forget!

Lucy Binns (10)
New Lodge School

The Little Lady

There once was a lady whose hair was pink
she had tied it and dyed it and washed it in the sink.
There the pink was stuck in her hair
she looked in the mirror and screamed with a scare!
The roots of her hair started turning red
so she fell on the bed as if she was dead.
But when she came to, she knew it was true,
her hair was totally red!
She ran to the bathroom again and again
in the end she took a pill which made her ill
and that was the end of her!

Chloe Buckland (8)
New Lodge School

Flowers

The first flower is a lily,
Some people think they're silly.

The second flower is a daisy,
Some say they're lazy.

The third flower is a rose,
Sometimes they look like bows.

The fourth flower is a poppy,
When people see them they go all soppy.

The fifth flower is a daffodil,
They always like standing still.

The sixth flower is a snowdrop,
But by the spring they start to flop.

The seventh flower is a bluebell,
They have a very delicate smell.

Harriet Barton (9)
New Lodge School

The Monkeys

T he monkeys leap from tree to tree,
H appy in the jungle they are glad to be,
E verlasting talent for swinging.

M onkeys never get bored of chattering.
O n the branches they love to hang,
N ever in danger of slipping or falling.
K ings of the jungle they are to me.
E ating bananas ripe and tasty,
Y ellow, yummy bunches, a treetop feast.
S wung out and dozing after a long day!

Lily Akerman (8)
New Lodge School

Overrun With Kangaroos!

The plain was derelict, dark, at peace
No creature slithered or moved, all noise had ceased
When suddenly a brown group jumped frantically across the hot plain
No lion could stop them, even with a huge mane
Then a huge mob grew to a massive mob, then a ginormous mob
Like a brown custard of legs!
As the kangaroos trampled across flowers and flattened trees
Even the bees said they weren't pleased.
The cheetahs just ran for their lives
They were as heartless as flies
As the deer ran past
But they were so fast and quickly they passed
Then all of the kangaroos in a bunch
Sprang for the hunters
While they were having lunch!
Lions, tigers, jackals too,
As battle commenced!
The ants thought they had sensed
The anteater had collided with a fence
The hunters were no match
Because the kangaroos fought in a batch!
King Lion shouted above the noise,
'Tally ho, boys!'
The plain could be at peace
If they gave the *Webb Ellis Cup* back!

Matthew Eagers (10)
New Lodge School

Overrun By Spiders

In the fields of England,
So peaceful and calm,
The spiders are tiny
And cause no one harm.
They live secret lives,
In the depth of the night,
Leaving dew-covered webs
In the cool morning light.

But spiders abroad leave me feeling quite ill,
They're large and they're hairy
Having bites that can kill.
If in the country I happen to roam
I'm very much safer with spiders at home.

The point I am making
In this little rhyme,
Is these 'foreign' spiders
Come one at a time.
It's true that they're frightening,
But rare to see one.
But in England, by spiders
We're quite overrun!

Alexander Heuvel (10)
New Lodge School

The Four Seasons

In the winter
It is cold
Snow falls from the sky
People go sledging
Plants look dead

In the spring
Little buds appear on the plants and start to grow
Everything looks green again
A bright, fresh green
Yellow daffodils shine brightly

In the summer
People like to go on holiday
Children paddle in the sea
Parents sit on the beach and read the newspaper
It is a good time for picnics

In the autumn
Leaves turn red, orange and brown
The wind blows
Leaves fall from the trees
The shops are full of Christmas things.

Ryan Winter (9)
New Lodge School

Overrun By Snails

In my house when all was quiet,
Loads of snails came in and started a riot.
Down the chimney, out the chair,
Through the window, in my hair.

Under the carpet, in the shed,
Up the stairs and in my bed.
Through the floorboards, in the lock,
Smashing the door down, one's in my sock!

In the front hall, down the sink,
And now they're sliming on my mink.
If they don't go, I'm going to die,
When they're gone, I can heave a big sigh.

Sliming along like a loud and gooey frog,
They are not fluffy like my pet dog.
I was just sleeping when woken by beeping,
Slime on my arm, the beeping's the alarm.

Now they are drying
They are all dying . . .
A blanket of salt fell over their head,
They've perished, they're gone, now they're dead!

Greg van Staden (10)
New Lodge School

Overrun With Ants

The house was silent, dark, at peace,
No movement outside, all noise had ceased
When suddenly . . .
An army of ants scuttled down the stairs
Some even crawled up my flares!
They swarmed in the kitchen
Looking for food
I was in a right old mood.
I brushed them away
My brother said, 'It's OK'
I rang 999 to ask for help
When I heard the dog starting to yelp
The ants were nibbling at his paws
They rushed upstairs
Invading beds and chairs
They then escaped from the house
And scurried next door
I heard a scream
A shout, a roar . . .
Then silence!

Sophie Lee (9)
New Lodge School

Overrun With Gorillas

The house was silent, dark, at peace
No movement outside, all noise had ceased
When suddenly . . .
While I was watching TV
A gorilla, jumped out at me
There were one, two, three, four
I fell to the floor
As they broke down the door
Lean, mean, tough and scary
Their long arms dangled
Flea-ridden and hairy
They chased me to the kitchen
Through the living room
To the bathroom, in the shower
Back to the first room
I switched on the TV
They looked at me
And begged for food
Then realised they were rude
When they were done
Having eaten their grub
They looked fat and plump
So I found a knife and fork
Ooh! They tasted like pork.

Christopher Ede (10)
New Lodge School

Cub In The Cupboard!

There's a cub in the cupboard
What could it be?
Maybe a sly fox or a chimpanzee!

It's scratching on the doors
It could be a boar!
Maybe . . .

A cub in the cupboard
He's lying on a cloth
Maybe he's scratched himself
Or could it be a moth?

He comes out of the cupboard
He starts looking around
When he comes out
He falls on the ground.

He starts coming closer,
He hears my dad's motor
Arriving at the house.
He looks around and thinks
Could it be a mouse?

So there's a cub in the cupboard
What could it be?
Maybe a sly fox or a chimpanzee!

Mackenzi Inouye
New Lodge School

Bother And Dash

I like the look of lots of things
So it's difficult to choose
My mum says I can only have one thing
And I really need new shoes.

'But Mummy,
I just want to have some fun
I'd rather buy sweets, some cakes,
And a big sticky bun!'

'The shoes you've got,' Mum said
'Are *so* not right
They're worn at the toe
And *ever so* tight!'

'But I can manage
With the shoes I'm wearing
So what if they're scruffy
And the laces are tearing?

Mummy!
I don't care if they let in rain
I've said it once
And I'll say it again.
I'll stamp my feet
Oh bother and dash
It's just a waste of my time
And a waste of your cash!'

Ellis Clarke (9)
New Lodge School

Overrun With Pigeons

The street was silent, dark, at peace,
No movement outside, all noise had ceased
When suddenly . . .
The pigeons flew to the centre,
Tender wings flapping all over,
They danced,
They pranced,
Rat-like fat things.
Some feathery, some scary,
Some leave white goo,
'Please next time, use the loo.'
But when you want them to go,
Come up behind and shout,
'Boo!'

Camilla Froy (10)
New Lodge School

Harvey The Hedgehog

Harvey the hedgehog is a good old fellow,
He likes to sleep with his little Toto.

Toto is a cute, small cat,
He always has on his head a hat.

Toto is a fluffy toy,
Harvey says he's not a girl, he's a boy.

Harvey has spikes on his back,
So the animals will not attack.

Harvey is not real, you see,
He and Toto are toys, which belong to me.

Harvey the hedgehog is a good old fellow,
He likes to sleep with his little Toto.

Eddy Buckpitt (9)
New Lodge School

Mrs MacGinty

Mrs MacGinty's horse,
Was grey and dappled of course

His legs, long and strong
As they carried her along
In a joyful rush of pure feeling

Then came a sad day
While fetching some hay
She found him looking glum and quite lonely

She dug deep
Until she found a sweet
Yes, just a single candy!

Now each new day
In his own special way
Her pocket he searches quite gladly!

Daisy Combridge (10)
New Lodge School

Winter

Freezing cold
Icy fingertips
Slippery pavements
Can't ride my bike
Build a snowman
Carrot for a nose
Coal for his eyes
Pipe in his mouth
Smiley face
Big tummy
When the weather turns warmer
The snowman melts
He's gone forever.

Bradley Fenn (7)
Priory School

The Boy With A Mind

Oh, I'm a very bad boy with a lack of control
So when I'm excited, on the floor I roll.
Over and under and under and over,
I hear my mother shouting, 'Think, boy, *control!'*

'Mum, Mum, Larry's out of control again.'
My little brother thinks I'm insane.
Round and round and up and down,
Dad is shouting at me with an awful frown.

My doctor thinks I'm mad,
My friends think I'm sad.
Left and right and right and left,
I'm just out of control.

I suck slimy snot,
I crack my mum's pot.
Crash and smash and smash and crash,
All without a care in the world.

Oh, I'm a very bad boy with a lack of control
So when I'm excited, on the floor I roll.
Over and under and under and over,
I hear my mother shouting, 'Think boy, *control!'*

Naveen Kumar (10)
Priory School

Winter

I like mice
I like rice
I like to freeze
I like to eat cheese
I like snow
I hate the flow
I like frogs
I hate logs
I can't wait till
January!

Stephen Rice (8)
Priory School

Winter

Children are outside in the snow
Throwing snowballs in the air.
Their knees are cold
Their knees are like ice
They are scampering around
Just like mice!

Frogs are jumping on the logs
Chasing after people's dogs
The wind is blowing
And it's snowing
The light is glowing
Icicles are growing.

The snow is melting
But more snow will come.
Animals hibernate
Children open the gate
And have snowball fights beneath the streetlights.

Jem Wraith (8)
Priory School

Mice In Ice

When I was walking down the road I saw some ice
In the ice were some mice,
Next to the mice was some rice.
Next to the rice was a dice.
I walked more
And I saw
Three more
Mice in ice.

Jack Butt (7)
Priory School

Hope

Some people don't have hope,
Like circus men hanging off a rope.
Some people get all the cheer,
But some drink all of the beer.
Some children are in a maths test,
When some are having a rest.
Hope is a remarkable feeling,
Not like cards in a poker dealing.
Hope is great and wonderful,
You should have it in a swimming pool.
There are some children who don't have a home,
When there are emperors who live in Rome.
God is with you all the day,
So don't stop, go all the way.
You must support your friends,
But don't guide them into a dead end.
So don't forget to have hope,
For life is not a joke.

William Braterman (10)
Priory School

The Snow

The snow is bright
Bright white
Cold as a freezer
If you don't have a coat
Get one *now!*
Christmas is coming to town
Ice, ice!
This is ice -
Hard and slippery
It is *fun!*

Craig Short (7)
Priory School

Fix It!

Fix the joints,
And the rail track points,
The gears,
And look at those dears,
The rotors,
Boy, listen to the motors,
Keep them whirring,
Purring,
Keep them smooth,
On the move,
In my groove,
Oh yeah! Oh yeah! Oh yeah!
We're on the move,
I've got my groove,
So you better move,
Oh yeah!

James Patston (11)
Priory School

Frost

The frost has come
And I'm here again
Oh, it's really cold
And the snow smells of gold
Oh! I love the snow!

Oh, it's time for the snow to settle
And the ice is as hard as metal.

The frost has come
And I'm here again
Oh, it's really cold
And the snow smells of gold
Oh! I love the snow!

Edward Price (7)
Priory School

The Fast Tortoise

There was a tortoise
Who carried his home all around the world

He went to . . .
England, France, America, Canada, Australia, Africa,
All around the world

When he went to England
He met a robin

When he went to France
He met a snail

When he went to America
He met the President

When he went to Canada
He met a beaver

When he went to Australia
He met a kangaroo

When he went to Africa
He met a lion

He went to Banstead
And lived right next to Priory School

Then he hibernated
And went to sleep.

Ryon Head (8)
Priory School

In The Crowd

People get mad
In the crowd,
Their heads pop with rage.

Once I got kicked in the head.
At the hospital after the football match
My parents thought I was dead.
The man who kicked me didn't apologise
Just laughed.

When I found out I needed an operation
To me it seemed like a situation
Of life and death.

Days went by
But I still felt pain,
Why?

Suddenly
I woke up
Then I dreaded everything
No longer.
Finding out it was a dream
I felt stronger.
It was a relief to find out that I could walk
And that I could properly talk.

I went downstairs to breakfast
And then my father joined me
He told me
That we were going to a
Football match!

Charlie Stebbings (9)
Priory School

My Pet Crocodile

My pet crocodile liked to sit in the water and bath
And his name was Mr McCath
He went munch, munch
And made a big crunch
He ate my Action Man once
For his lunch, it was yummy
He was fat
He looked like a cat
He ran away
And came back the next day
He ate everything in the bin
And made an awful din
We went off to the park
And saw a grey shark
And whilst we were there
He ran away and gave us all a scare
When we went back to our house
We saw a hairy mouse
I called the council, they came in
But they were so scared when they saw our croc
They jumped in the bin
Our crocodile made friends with the mouse
But the next day there was a murder in the house . . . !

Joseph Stevens (8)
Priory School

Animal Poem

I had two orange fish
My cat took a lucky dip
And now I've got one!

The monster was hot
He ran so fast and got so tired
That he flopped!

Jamie Budgett (8)
Priory School

Thoughts About My Life

Holidays are
long days and late nights playing out
cycling, riding and running about.

Ice cream is
a touch of frost in the summertime,
a melting mountain of chocolate slime.

My pets are
part of the family to me
we run and play and giggle with glee.

Magic tricks are
mysterious and amazingly cunning
and when I do them the effects are stunning.

The first day of term is
as fresh and new as the morning
but by the last day of term, I'm tired and yawning.

Francis Hudson (11)
Priory School

My Pet Dragon

My pet dragon ate a bird
And put the toast on the fire
If you get a pet dragon
Make sure he lights the fire

If you get a pet dragon
And want to look after it
Give him plenty to eat
Coal, wood and sausage meat.

Rhys Melville (8)
Priory School

Second Floor

'Sir, Bill and Ben are fighting
On the second floor
Now they will be lighting
A candle, I am sure.'

'Stop, stop, stop
Please, please, please
You're going to melt the lock and keys.'

'Right, that's it!
You start striding
Think I'm a twit
Well, don't try hiding.

The only way to handle you lot
Is to send you to the chief
And no excuses like 'I'm too hot'
Or pretend your name is Keith.

Now you two, what have you done?
Smashed a glass, broken a desk or had a fight?'
'Nothing Sir, just having fun
And playing with a light.'

James Burke (11)
Priory School

My Pet Rabbit

My pet rabbit was very, very clever
My pet rabbit had a strange little feather
My pet rabbit was found in space
He dropped out of his aircraft and landed in a place
The place was called France
The rabbit's name was Lance.

My pet rabbit!

Jack Thoroughgood (8)
Priory School

The Storm

The rain is pouring down,
The sea is rising, higher and higher,
The flowers are going to die
And the planes, they cannot fly.
Houses are collapsing
The skies are getting black,
The ducks are going quack! Quack! Quack!
The ship is going to blow.
The storm is getting worse and worse,
It's never going to end.
As I look outside my window
Everything is a mess.
I just want to stop it now -
I think I just saw a flying cow.
I see people crying
And praying for help,
My mum is sitting with me,
Finally I drift off to sleep and wake up next morning.
I look outside my window
One more time,
Everything is still damp and wet
But the sun has come out.

Jordan Lipman (9)
Priory School

My Pet Crocodile

My pet crocodile goes *chomp! Chomp! Chomp!*
When he was young he lived in a swamp
He was feared by animals alike
Even the world's biggest pike
Then one day I took him to school
He spent all day in the swimming pool
All the kids ran out of the room
They thought he would bring them to their doom!

Matthew Clark (9)
Priory School

Santa's Little Elves

Once Santa gets all his toys
Back to his boys
They will start working all the hours they can.

And for that simple one-night ride
Their names are thanked far and wide.
Now it is fair you and your friends
Have to go and say a prayer.

These little guys who make the toys
That Santa gives to girls and boys
Think that it will not be wrong
To sing a song while Santa's gone.

Let's sing to these special elves
Bill, Harry, Charlie, Roger, Willie and Mary!

Charles Stairs (11)
Priory School

My Journey

Today I'm not going to any old place,
I am going to outer space.
I'll land on the moon,
Eat stars with a spoon.
I'll land on Mars,
And scoff all the chocolate bars.
Next Jupiter is my landing spot,
And I'll take a great, big pot.
I'll use that pot for a drink,
I got it from under the kitchen sink.
Now for home, away,
What a journey I've had today.

Peter Henley (9)
Priory School

The Dog Called Everest!

(He can speak!)

There was a dog called Everest
He said he was insane
He ran up Mount Everest
And hummed this on his way
'And up and up and up and up'
And when he got to the top
He put the flag on it
He fell down Mount Everest
And hummed this on his way
'And down and down and down and down'
And people cheered him on his way
'Hooray . . . hooray . . . hooray to doggy'
And that's how he got his bone.

Ben Askew (8)
Priory School

The Robin

A red and brown robin is so small,
It is round, just like a tiny ball!
Its small, soft wings
Are brown and black
And its voice is smooth for singing.
It flies so high,
And spins around in the sky.
His little beak
Is smooth and sleek.
Its chest is red and much
Bigger than its head.
It often has good food to eat
And sits on its log and goes to sleep.

Christopher Bolton (9)
Priory School

Panic!

This is the time when you have to panic
A tornado is coming right at you
It's whirling and whirling and whirling around

And you're very, very afraid
Sometimes you think
That you can't even blink
Because it's whirling and whirling and whirling around

You're shivering and shivering
Your life is in danger
You are in danger
Your life is hanging on the last piece of a thin thread
Because it's whirling and whirling and whirling around.

Rakesh Joshi (9)
Priory School

Of What Am I Scared?

I was having a snowball fight,
When suddenly a snowball hit me.

It cut me,
And there I saw a piece of ice stuck on my forehead,
My friends pulled it out,
It was shiny and full of blood.

I put some white snow on my forehead,
And it felt so cool,
The snow gradually taking away the blood,
I took the snow off,

And found that there was such a
Beautiful colour contrast
Between the white fresh snow
And the dribbly blood.

Nirav Patel (11)
Priory School

Storm

I'm standing in the storm on my lawn
With wind in my face, it's time to pace to a shelter
People shouting, 'Stop! Stop!'
But the storm just keeps going on
I say to myself 'When the storm is over,
The world will be better.'
When I see people shout, it puts me out.

When I wake up each morning,
I say, 'Has it stopped yet?' But the answer is *no!*
I feel the boom in my wits; it's driving me insane
Every bit more, it's driving me poor
When it finishes, I hope I'm alive
I can taste the rain, it's a pain.

It's going to stop, I can sense it
You can say, 'I love it, I love it!'
But I think it's rubbish.

Daniel Herbert (10)
Priory School

Cliffs

Cliffs are colossal
Cliffs are cavernous
Cliffs are lethal
Even these days.
Some abseil for a sport
And sometimes even fall.
From a helicopter some cliffs look like the Earth's mouth.
Some get deeper every day
Some stay as they may.

Daniel Westwood (10)
Priory School

Panic Attack

Panic is a way of life,
It helps you on the way to greatness.
Panic is a way of life,
It's like a very big, sharp knife.
One big feeling inside your mind,
What you must do is not stay behind.
Don't be scared, don't run away,
But don't think of trying to stay.

Panic is a way of life,
It's running through your blood,
But it's not a way of life - is it?
Or is it not?
Don't ask me just ask yourself,
If you get scared you will lose your health.
Remember . . .
Panic attack is *not* a way of life.

Arran Weeraratne (10)
Priory School

Could It Be A Dream?

Cornered.
The class had ratted me out.
Freddy, Teddy and Massy
All angry with me.
Had I done a bad thing?
Was breaking a pencil
A bad thing?
I wished and wished it was a dream
But alas, it's not
Or is it? *Bang!*
I woke up, it was just a dream or was it?

Chris Beale (9)
Priory School

Thunderstorm

The storm comes from the distance
The wind begins to howl
It's the middle of the night
The storm comes closer
Like a bounding wolf.
The lightning brightens up the sky
And thunder starts to rumble.

But I am safe inside
Whilst the storm gathers overhead.
Will it ever go away?
How did the storm come so fast?

But suddenly . . .
The storm left
But I am still terrified
Will it come back again -
Or will it still blow on through the night?

Thomas Williams (9)
Priory School

Storm

The storm is really rapid
The children could not sleep
The thunder was as strong as a tiger
And the sound was like a lion roaring.
The boats were swinging to and fro
The storm was getting worse and worse
And now the rain was pouring down
And all the dogs started to bark.
Puddles were rising and rising
Now the houses were starting to flood.
Just as everything was going haywire
A sun comes out and everything is back to normal
That that was the end of the sun.

Henry Miller (9)
Priory School

The Outdoor World

The outdoor world, what a place,
An inspirational place without a name,
As the birds swoop overhead,
It gives you a wonderful feeling.

The peace and quiet,
Or the roar of the long motorway,
Climbing trees and making towers,
The gentle streams and the spring flowers.

All the meadows stretch far and wide,
Beautiful red and blue skies,
The washing waves telling lies,
And the tall Canadian Redwoods whispering secrets to your face.

But we should respect Mother Nature,
Before there is a major disaster,
Already the mighty blue whale is dying off,
Because of crude oil spills.

Before we think of going to Mars,
And the far away distant stars,
We should think of our planet first,
What a place after all, with the beautiful waterfall.

The thing about the outside world,
Is that natural and industrial things can come together,
In rain or fog or sleet or snow,
Never mind the weather though.

And this, of course, brings my poem to an end,
About the Earth on which our life depends,
God bless the world, what a beautiful place,
And everybody in the human race.

William Broad (10)
Priory School

The Perfect Place

There's a place in your heart
For India to grow,
Where the hungry are fed
By the wealthy alone

Your eyes start to water
As you start to raise your head,
You see the sparkling water
Shining round your four-poster bed

You see the Himalayas
As tall as can be
With water dripping down the mountainside.

You start pumping your legs
As you see the Taj Mahal,
Up, up you go
As it towers above your head.

As the water flows
The spirits of the Ganges blow
People are crying
Putting loved ones' ashes in the water.

There's a place in your heart
For India to grow,
Where the hungry are fed
By the wealthy alone.

Priyam Patel (11)
Priory School

Class 109

'Sir, Sir, Jimmy's got Bob and Bob's punching Dave
Is there anything you can do to make them behave?'
Class 109 are trouble
If I were a teacher I'd get there on the double.
They punch, they kick
They're not afraid to flick.
The headmaster's no use
They'll think of an excuse.
Parents are called in,
Oh what a din.
The noise spreads around the school,
Some kids think it's cool.
Their homework is atrocious,
Class 109 are ferocious.
What can be done?
They must learn to have fun.
As I write in my diary,
I'm so glad I go to the Priory.

Colin Russell (10)
Priory School

Monster Who?

Monster, monster who?
We know whom!
Monster, monster who?
We know whom!

It's you!
It's you!

Luke Mellor (8)
Priory School

Cliff Tops

The cliff tops high, steep and rocky
Now and then I feel the breeze of the wind blowing in my face
'Honk! Honk!' I hear flocks of geese fly over my head.
I say to myself now and then, 'Good golly, I wish I could fly.'
The waves splash so high on the side of the cliff, they land on my face
Sometimes I can smell the salt sea.
If I feel cold I lie on the floor and curl up in a ball and
Look at the sky.
'I've got an idea,' I said
I gathered some bamboo and straw out in the fields
And I made a ladder, I tied it to a rock and a post
And climbed down it.
I could feel the water on my feet then *splash!* I splashed in the water.
It was freezing cold, I had a swim around and I felt warm
Soon I climb out and dry myself and go home.
On the way home I think I've had a great time.

Joseph Hillyard   (9)
Priory School

Force 9

I'm queuing up for a roller coaster,
I'm with my friend (he's such a boaster),
I'm feeling really, really scared,
I'm only doing this because I was dared.

I'm nearly on the ride,
I think I'd rather die,
The ride is called Force 9
Everyone else is fine.

People call me a scaredy-cat,
Boy, it's hot, I should have brought a hat!
Anyway, what do they know?
Please don't make me go!

Calum Stone   (11)
Priory School

In The Jungle

In the jungle,
It's dark and scary,
Everything's fierce,
And very hairy!

The monkeys swing,
From tree to tree,
Making trouble,
Wherever they may be!

A bird sings,
Then a lion roars,
I'm glad I'm not squashed,
Beneath his paws!

The trees are tall,
And covered in mould,
I bet that they had
Done as they were told!

I then fall over,
On my head,
And then wake up,
In my own bed!

John Whelton (10)
Priory School

Cliff Top, Cliff Top

The high cliff top
Looks like a ragged piece of clothing,
The sea crashing against the bottom of the cliff.
The sea was as beautiful as a blue diamond crystal.

Chistopher Russell (9)
Priory School

Tiger Strike

The tiger: I see my prey
I'm not allowed here
But I come as I may,
I lurk in the shadows,
I see him moving ounce by ounce
I'm ready to pounce!

The gazelle: My killer is here
Killing me and my young, I fear
I gather my young up
They don't want to go, I say, 'Shut up!'

The gazelle: We start running, quick!
It's like running on a candlewick
I think I'm going to die
Oh why? Oh why?

The tiger: I've gone out to get him
It is easy as he is so dim
I heave him up and start moving
I get back home and am really shattered
My cubs are absolutely flattered!

The tiger: After we'd all eaten the meat
We decided to go to sleep
I lay down exhausted
Tomorrow is a new day
Tomorrow I will play.

George Chesser (11)
Priory School

Sports Are Great

There are lots of sports in the world.
All sorts of things like football, cricket and rugby.
You can jump and run,
And burn off last night's cinnamon bun.
Sports started in the past,
And it's extremely quick and fast.
In cricket you need a bat,
And you need a funny-looking hat.
And then you throw the ball,
It's an advantage if you're tall.
Then if you're out someone calls
'Howzat?'
Football is loved by all,
There are 11 players and 1 ball.
Running in and out, jumping up and down.
When I lose, I moan and frown.
Golf is a quiet sport.
It's hard to play but easily taught.
Rugby is a great game,
I think rugby's a great name.
In rugby you can get quite muddy,
The other team aren't your buddies.
Although the scrum can be quite fun,
You can sometimes land on your bum.
When I swim I feel free,
I splish and splash and say, 'Yippee!'
I love sports, it's plain to see,
So why not come and join me?

Luke McCormack (11)
Priory School

Winter

Whilst the mice skates on ice
A very gentle breeze comes along
The mice tries to scram
But when one of them sneezes
They all fall down.
I walk away
I feel a snowball hit my back
I try to run away
But find it very hard
I struggle
But whilst I struggle, it starts to snow
The boys start to go and I decide to go home
And have a nice cup of coffee.

William Townsend (7)
Priory School

Monsters

Monsters are bad
Monsters are mad
Monsters are crazy
And also very lazy.

Monsters are scary
And very, very hairy
Not very sleepy
But very creepy.

Monsters have a huge appetite
And always think they're right
But I won't run
I think they're fun.

Joshua Aarons (7)
Priory School

Storm

Storms are brilliant,
Storms are physically dominant,
There're strips of lightning,
That fall from the blue.

It zaps the treetops,
Metal too,
I wouldn't unlock a window
When a storm is here.

I wouldn't go outside,
It's too cold
Nor in a swimming pool
I could die.

They're a zigzag shape,
Like Harry Potter's scar.
But not going down,
Going across like a car.

A storm is a mix up,
Of thunder and lightning.
Which makes the sea rough,
And the rain is the same.

When a storm is here,
Houses are clear.
Mix with fire,
Can make a detonation.

Storms are strong,
Do not got outside.

Kemi Chaggar (10)
Priory School

Hope

The light is dim
and this is grim.
It's very cold
but I'm keeping hold,
and there's still hope!

I haven't a dime
and I've done no crime,
I don't move a lot,
for my life I have to plot.
Is there much hope?

I stay awake some nights
and have some fights,
alas, why did this storm come to me -
for I have nowhere to flee?
I hope there's hope.

Jack Sayle (9)
Priory School

Winter

Once it was winter,
It was full of ice,
The mice ran
Into the house.
The snow is bad
The crow was angry.
The old man liked to eat
His cheese
In the breeze.
The trees are blowing,
Waters flowing.
Fire's on,
Light's on.
The blizzards are coming,
The wizard is coming.

Rocco Birri (8)
Priory School

Brave Heart

Freedom, freedom!
Will wants freedom.
Fight, fight
Fight for freedom.
William wants to be free,
He wants to die with honour.

Brave Will, brave Will,
William Wallace.
Dying for freedom.
He wants to be free,
People want to be free.
Freedom is the best, freedom is the best,
Will loves freedom,
People love freedom.
Dying for freedom,
That's so brave.

I would like to hear the footsteps of William,
I would like to understand the word freedom.
I would like to have a word freedom in my mind.

Feel how good freedom is,
A word starting with *F* stands for freedom.

Jong Yoon Song (11)
Priory School

Storm

The storm is furious
It roars at night,
Deadly!

Bluff! Roar!
Bluff! Roar!
The wind blows hard,
Pushing you away
One step back.

You try to have a fight,
But you can't even hit it.

The sun emerges
The dark wind has vanished
The sun's beam
Comes out at last.
It sparkles and glows
It is gone -
Our biggest foe.

Sultaz Ijaz (9)
Priory School

The Storm

I was by the window
Looking outside at the gloom of the night
When flash lightning hit the road.
Then I saw the sea, the rough sea.

Crashing against the shore,
I went outside to see
What the noise was.
It was raining cats and dogs,
I shivered like a penguin,
Then I woke up but I didn't know why I felt so cold.

Guy Mason (10)
Priory School

Earthquake Panic

When an earthquake flattened our house
We ran, we screamed, we didn't have time to grab our things.
'Run for your lives!' shouted the neighbours to each other.
'Nothing's more important!'
When we were running, I saw a man -
He wasn't running.
Why? I thought,
His shirt was caught and
He couldn't run.
It seemed as if his legs were waving for help.
I thought hard, *can I help! If so, how?*
I got his shirt and set him free.
He said, 'Thank you!'
And he ran off like a flash.
Even if you panic, there are some things you can do.

So Okubo (10)
Priory School

Christmas

Stay up late
Can't sleep
Santa comes
Stockings filled
Snow outside
Ice on the pond
Turkey for dinner
Presents to unwrap
Chocolates on the tree
Games to play
Relations visit
Christmas is great.

James Rhodes (7)
Priory School

Panic

Panic is in the air,
Cars are bumper to bumper.
We're late!
What will teacher say?
We're in trouble,
What will we do?
There's a traffic jam at the traffic lights,
Yes, lights change. Brum! Brum! Off we go!
Coming up to the school roundabout -
No, not roadworks!
Got to be at school in three minutes.
Yes! Just made it, the bell's just about to go.
Bye Mum.

Matthew Stannard (9)
Priory School

The Snow

I love the snow
I love the snow
It's so white and so soft,
You can make snowmen and
Have snowball fights with your
Family and friends.
Most of all
Enjoy the snow -
Play with it
Have fun with it
Enjoy it!

Luke Marder (8)
Priory School

Poem

Cliff top, hill top makes a buzzy stream
And the hilltop is just fabulous.
It also has a waterfall which crashes against the rocks
It wears away the pebbles in one single shot!

And the cliff top is snow-capped for snowy skiers
Which go up and down with their snowy bears.
The bears go nuts but they are brainy
They have nothing to do except go crazy!
They go mad once you call them, they run at your like a fierce dog!
Helicopters are in the air and fire is everywhere
People are getting mad because the Fire Brigade isn't on time
People run in all directions, but they have no chance.

Nial Ahmad (10)
Priory School

Fear

What are you frightened of?
I'm afraid of heights
I would be terrified
If I was lifted up by kites.

Fear is a terrible thing
But everyone has some.
It is when you're scared of something
And don't know what to do.

Fear keeps on coming back
You can get it any day
Sometimes you dream it at night
But in the end, it goes away.

George Hutchins (10)
Priory School

In Old China

In old China there lived a miner who lived on Valley Road,
Well in fact, he's quite fat as everybody knows.
He eats green beans in the middle of Mass, which everyone has seen
But by far the worst thing he ever did, was to fill his pockets
                                                    with cream.

He never cares what anyone says
He just cares about his food.
His wife is nice and often thinks
The wonderful thing is he cannot sing.
He drinks green tea each day at three
And then eats jelly and cakes.
He tries to speak but no use you see
His mouth is jammed shut with food.
I think that's kind of cute, don't you?
But some people think he's rude!

Katie Wise (7)
St Francis' Catholic Primary School, Caterham-On-The-Hill

Feelings

My heart is as cold as stone,
I'm feeling chilled to the bone.

My knees feel weak
And my mouth won't speak.

My head feels dizzy
And my hair feels frizzy.

Laura Jackson (8)
St Francis' Catholic Primary School, Caterham-On-The-Hill

Love Falls

Love above - February is the month of love!

Love is from above; it comes with a dove
And flies above.

Love comes as a beat - it shoots at your feet.
It makes your heart warm, your body transform.

Her hair is gold, her eyes are blue,
I wonder if she has a clue?

The dove above is sending love.
It falls upon her doors.

Run, skip and jump - it makes my heart thump!
The sun makes me glow - does my love show?
It's like climbing a tree it sets me free.

So let's go with the flow and make up a show,
And show the harp's bow.
So come on, Cupid, shoot your arrow
Please make sure your aim is narrow.

Draw your bow tight, let her know tonight
That our love is right . . .
My love is in sight.

Daniel Mangan (8)
St Francis' Catholic Primary School, Caterham-On-The-Hill

Winter Wonder

W ind whistling through the window.
 I ce that is covering the cars.
N umbness that is felt on fingers.
T emperature that regularly hits zero
E erie silence in the snow.
R ace of the bobsleighs, racing in the snow.

Isabelle O'Connor (8)
St Francis' Catholic Primary School, Caterham-On-The-Hill

Mums

We need our mums,
They're our best chums.
A shoulder to cry on
An arm to lie on.

Some mums are cuddly and soft, like teddy bears,
Mum gives you big hugs to show that she cares.
Some mums take us out to eat
Sometimes just for a treat.
Some mums take you out to shop
Just to buy you a fancy frock.
Some mums buy you sweets galore
Come on now *she's not a bore!*
The best thing is . . . we love our mummies . . .
Because we came out of their tummies.
And to my mum I'd like to say -
Loveable and kind, you will always stay.
I'll try and make up for all she's done,
But just for now I want to say, 'Thank you Mum!'

Chantelle Lindsay (10)
St Francis' Catholic Primary School, Caterham-On-The-Hill

On A Summer's Day

On a summer's day
When the wind whistled
And the trees rustled.
With a ripple in the pond
And someone crying
With someone rhyming
And the war began
On a summer's day.

Madeleine Barter (10)
St Francis' Catholic Primary School, Caterham-On-The-Hill

The Future 2

What will there be left?
Will there be TV?
What will there be?

Will there be any animals?
Will there? Will there?
Will there be any school? No!

Will there be people left?
Will there? Will there?
Will there be food?

Will there be evil teachers?
I really hope not!
Will there be houses left?

Will there be any work?
Will there be any pollution?
Will there? Will there?

Will there be PlayStations?
Will there be computers?
Will there? Will there?

Will there be Earth?
Will there? Will there?
Will there be anything?

David Pullinger (8)
St Francis' Catholic Primary School, Caterham-On-The-Hill

Puppies

I love puppies
They are cute
They are fluffy
They are funny
But they like it best
When I rub their tummy.

Holly Brown (8)
St Francis' Catholic Primary School, Caterham-On-The-Hill

Rumble

There's a rumble in the jungle that
I haven't heard before.
It's over in the trees and I can't
Bear it anymore.

There's a hissing and a swishing
And a swaying in the trees, if
I close my eyes - make it disappear, please.

There's a rumble in the jungle
That I haven't heard before, it's
Getting closer and it sounds
Like a roar.

There's a snapping and a flapping
Down by my knees, it's swirling
And curling and going to make
Me sneeze.

There's a rumble in the jungle
That I haven't heard before.
It's a grumble or a mumble I
Can't really be sure.

There's a shadow on the floor
The clock is chiming loudly,
It's saying half-past four.

There's a reason for this rumble
And all the noise, it's the grumble
In my tummy, saying 'Mummy,
It's time for tea and I want it now please!'

Ciara Mockett (8)
St Francis' Catholic Primary School, Caterham-On-The-Hill

If . . .

If I won the lottery, I would buy myself a car.
If I found a secret treasure, I would buy
a palace in a land, afar.

If I were to climb a tree, I would see the
world from sea to sea.
If I bought a big chocolate bar I would share
it with just you and me.

If I walked in a field of daisies, I would pick one
for every child, everywhere.
If I did all of these things, then I would
be the happiest person in the world.

Emily Ingram (10)
St Francis' Catholic Primary School, Caterham-On-The-Hill

Summer Love

I see you walking on the beach
As I see you
You make me want to screech

I see you playing in the sand
I wish that was you and me
Walking together hand in hand

I see you as a beautiful white dove
And I really miss
Your summer love.

Lydia Cebreiro (10)
St Francis' Catholic Primary School, Caterham-On-The-Hill

The Secrets Of The Sea

There's a big commotion
Down in the ocean.
There's all types of creatures,
Scattered around in the blue.
Mermaids with their scaly tails
And big blubbery, killer whales.
Don't miss these dazzling things
And for the dolphin that beautifully sings.
The eye-catching colours of an angel fish,
But make sure you don't become a swordfish dish.
The octopus wraps his arms around you
You may not see him in the deep, dark blue.
As you go down, it gets dark, dark, dark
Watch out! Don't be eaten by a shark!
Boats sail across the lighthouse as a guide;
The tide gently rocks the boat from side to side.
Some boats pollute the sea
We must stop it, you and me!

Ciara Bruget & Shannon Norman (9)
St Francis' Catholic Primary School, Caterham-On-The-Hill

Kevin

There was a man called Kevin
Who died and went to Heaven.
He went to the gate,
God said he was late.
'You should have been here at seven!'

Andrew Stevens (9)
St Francis' Catholic Primary School, Caterham-On-The-Hill

Future

Will the world be better
Or will it be worse?
Will Einstein wake and make flying cars
Or NASA find life on Mars?
Will there be a wizard?
Will there be a witch?
To fly and fight the humans' dirty ditch.
Will movies become real?
Will humans still be there?
Or will this world just be a universe scare?
Well, we'll just have to wait and see
What the future will be.

Isabelle Nicol (9)
St Francis' Catholic Primary School, Caterham-On-The-Hill

Me And My Dog

Me and my dog are barking mad.
We like to run and play.
When we are sad we lie in bed all day.
The next day we are glad . . .
Then we say 'Hooray!'

When I am at school my dog is unhappy.
When I come back from school he begins to drool.
The next day he is yappy.
Having a dog is very cool.

Emily Pemberton (7)
St Francis' Catholic Primary School, Caterham-On-The-Hill

Will There . . .

Will there be school
And definitely mass?
Will there be me
And my old friend, Cass?

Will there be Santa
With his big sack?
Will there be sweets?
Oh! I hope that they will be back!

Will there be breakfast
And will there be space?
Will there be air?
I'd be dead in that case!
Will there be anything, anything at all?

Rocio Crispin (7)
St Francis' Catholic Primary School, Caterham-On-The-Hill

My Future

What will the future be?
Will there be a war
Or will all living things
Fall down on the floor?

What will the future be?
Will you say bye to your mate?
Will war be over
Or will it be too late?

Emilio Crispin (9)
St Francis' Catholic Primary School, Caterham-On-The-Hill

My Poem

This is a poem about *me*
I hope you don't want to read about *me*
Because I'm hairy and scary
Ghostly and stare-e
You don't want to look at *me*
Because I'm green and mean
And I'm not to be seen

I am a goblin and my name is Soblin
Cos I sob and sob all day.

Elizabeth Madeleine Lawless (8)
St Francis' Catholic Primary School, Caterham-On-The-Hill

Batty Blood

I'm a batty little guy, big as a rat,
I'll suck the blood from your cat.
I'll sink my teeth into your skin,
No bat will find that's a sin.

Some will say my screech is worse than my bite,
But I also have no sight.

Alex Pullin (9)
St Francis' Catholic Primary School, Caterham-On-The-Hill

The Princess And Her Prince

The princess was in the high tower,
She was all alone.
Prince came by
On his horse.
He said, 'Let down your hair.'
And she did
Because she loved him.

Penny Brown (5)
St Francis' Catholic Primary School, Caterham-On-The-Hill

My Future

When I grow up, will there be apes?
When I grow up, will the world be here?
When I grow up, will there be a sapphire sky, astronomy,
The sea, the sparkling sea, glittering into your eyes?
When I grow up will anything change?
Will it not be polluted?
When I grow up I hope I'll be there.

Danica Driman (8)
St Francis' Catholic Primary School, Caterham-On-The-Hill

When I Went To The Park

When I went to the park on a cold winter's day
I wrapped up warm to go out and play.
When I got to the park I
Swung up and down on the swings,
Jumped on a plank that rings,
I climbed up the ladder and slid down the slide,
But when my mum called I went to go hide!

Mary Fothergill (8)
St Francis' Catholic Primary School, Caterham-On-The-Hill

Vampires

When a vampire appeared in the gloom,
He took me to my room,
He told me I must
Clean up all of the dust.
Then it will be his tomb!

Catherine Gibbons (8)
St Francis' Catholic Primary School, Caterham-On-The-Hill

Nursery Crimes!

Humpty Dumpty sat on the wall,
Humpty Dumpty had a great fall,
All the king's horses and all the king's men . . .
Ate him!

Jack and Jill
Went up the hill,
What's the use of that?
Jack fell down and broke his crown,
What a clumsy brat!

Four hot buns in a baker's shop,
Round and plump with a cherry on the top,
Along came Daniel with a penny one day,
Thought it was gross, and chucked it away!

Daniel Clackson (10)
St Martin's Junior School, Epsom

School!

We crept into the old, creaky house,
we saw bottles of goo,
we saw dead eyeballs on the floor,
it was school, it was school!

We went into the laboratory
where we saw dead bodies in a pool,
we saw rats' eyes and body bits,
it was school, it was school!

We ran out shaking,
our legs were quaking,
we never returned to that place,
school,
school,
school!

Haissam Adil (9)
St Martin's Junior School, Epsom

Seasons

Winter
A season of cold,
A season of snow,
Sitting by the fire, warm and snug.

Spring
A season of cleaning,
A season of daffodils,
Baby lambs are born!

Summer
A season of flowers,
A season of playing,
Sunbathing round the pool on holiday.

Autumn
A season of bonfires,
A season of fireworks,
Trees dropping their leaves to the ground.

All seasons are fun!

Jessica Chinchen (9)
St Martin's Junior School, Epsom

My Horse Misty!

My horse is as white as snow,
My horse is a great runner,
My horse is as soft as a feather,
My horse is as sweet as a foal,
My horse is also as cheeky as a monkey!

She is as gentle as a butterfly,
She is as funny as a jester,
Overall she is as cool as a DJ!

My horse is as fast as lightning,
My horse is as pretty as a flower,
My horse is also as fun as a playground.

Tessa Derry (10)
St Martin's Junior School, Epsom

An Old Kettle Of Fish

My sister is always
Driving me up the wall.
(I abseil back down.)

My mum says
That Dad has a finger in every pie.
(He wrecked them all.)

My uncle said
That I was swinging the lead.
(It was too heavy.)

My friend says
To hold your horses.
(They were too strong.)

My mum said
To hold your tongue.
(It was too slippery.)

My dad said
That my brother had his head in the clouds.
(He got awfully wet.)

My teacher said
That too many cooks spoil the broth.
(I don't like broth so that doesn't matter.)

Jonathan Hall (9)
St Martin's Junior School, Epsom

Witches Of The East

Frizzle
Frogs' eyes, bats' wings,
Spiders' toes, awful things
Snotty noses, snake's bite,
Watch out or we'll give you a fright!

Moonlight, moonlight of the sky,
Make all those children cry!
Ha, ha, ha, ha!

Goggles
Hallowe'en is one special time,
Where we cause violence and crime.
While you are having your happy dreams,
We'll wait until we hear your screams!

Moonlight, moonlight of the sky,
Make all those children cry!
Ha, ha, ha, ha!

Frizzle and goggles
We all like flying around.
We never touch the ground.
Our faces are all warty and green
When we fly at Hallowe'en!

Moonlight, moonlight of the sky,
Make all those children cry!
Ha, ha, ha, ha!

Jodie Rogers (9)
St Martin's Junior School, Epsom

I Hate School

No running in the corridors,
When you're typing never pause,
No talking in the hall,
Or using leather balls.

Now get on with your work,
When I'm shouting don't smirk,
No rude words in the playground,
Is it true that James just drowned?

No splashing in that puddle,
Or you will get in trouble,
Don't fiddle with your pencil case,
And boys don't play kiss-chase.

When it's the end of the day,
Go home and never play,
I don't get enough pay,
So *now go away!*

Matthew Thomas (11)
St Martin's Junior School, Epsom

Summertime Flowers

The blossom on the apple trees sparkle in the sun
While the bluebells in the field sway in the breeze.
The buttercups bloom and shimmer in the light
And then there's me, the rose, pink as can be.

The daisies hum their merry song
And dance in the warm, warm breeze,
While the snowdrops drop a splash of snow
And then there's me, the rose, pink as can be.

Briony Chandler (10)
St Martin's Junior School, Epsom

My Pet Hamster

I have a pet named Homer,
He's really, really cute.
He eats his food in big chunks.
He's a television on mute.

He's a feathery round ball.
He's an active little boy.
He's a small and poochy guy.
He's a bundle full of joy.

He's a running cheetah.
He's a lion with sharp teeth.
He's a terrified turtle.
He's a thin beige leaf.

I love Homer very much
And when he dies I'll be sad
But I'll enjoy him while he's alive.
He's the best pet I've ever had!

Francesca Jackson (9)
St Martin's Junior School, Epsom

My Fantasy Pet

My fantasy pet would be a dog crossed with a fish.
It would swim around in an enormous tank.
I'd buy the tank myself you see
(With money from my bank).

It would also grant a unicorn's horn.
It would grant my wishes too
And if you're very nice to it,
It might grant a wish for you.

I would love my fantasy pet.
I would love it day and night.
It might look like a monster though.
It could give my brother a fright.

Rebecca Pledge (9)
St Martin's Junior School, Epsom

I Know A Little Robin

I know a little robin
Who comes to play with me.
He lives out in my garden
In the great big apple tree.

I thought I'd call him 'Peanut'.
It seemed to suit him well
Because he liked to eat them
And leave behind the shell.

I love to watch him closely
When he stops for a little rest.
His tiny beak is really cute
But I like his red breast best.

Whenever we are digging
In the earth beside the swing,
He flies down to meet us
And hops proudly like a king.   .

He comes back every winter.
He really likes the snow.
He flies down to my window sill
And taps to let me know.

Before I go to school each day
I leave a tasty snack.
And thought I may not see him
I always see his tracks.

So if you see a robin
Tell him not to fly away.
Talk to him softly
For he only wants to play.

Emma Siggery (10)
St Martin's Junior School, Epsom

Cats

A round purring ball of contentment,
Or a hissing, spitting ball of resentment.

What are cats?

A rolling kitten, a ball of fluff,
A haughty adult that's had enough.

What are cats?

Lighted eyes, a rumbling purr,
Run your hand through its soft fur.

What are cats?

Tortoiseshell, tabby, black and calico,
Short-haired, long-haired and white as snow.

What are cats?

They make us think of royalty, of times past and gone.
They make us think of pharaohs, in their tombs alone.

What are cats?

Cats are fearsome creatures in the night,
Their eyes start to glow with a terrible light.

What are cats?

Look to the moon to see that cat's changing eye,
Situated high up there, bright in the sky.

What are cats?

Cats are a mystery,
A tragedy, a comedy.
A playful creature in daylight,
A terrible killer at night.

What are cats?

They are themselves.

Emma Woolgar (10)
St Martin's Junior School, Epsom

School For Year 3s

Big school is where you go
When you are only seven.
Most people are scared of it,
But some think it's Heaven!

The teachers stand there, looking down at you,
While big girls laugh behind your back.
The playground's giant and scary.
Your books are all in your sack.

The classroom's quite inviting,
But the teacher's looking mean.
She grabs you by the collar,
And cackles, 'Let's get you clean!'

The work is harder
Than the stuff in Year Two.
You start getting drowsy,
But still have lots to do.

Playtime's a relief,
But then the whistle blows.
Into the hall for assembly,
'What's assembly?' you ask.
They answer, 'Who knows?'

You nearly fall asleep in PHSE,
You've made a few friends, but golly!
Finally we get to go home,
Home under a brolly.

Emily Ranson (10)
St Martin's Junior School, Epsom

The Wanga Snake

Creeping through the jungle,
Parrots squawking,
Crocodiles snapping,
But nothing as deadly as the Wanga Snake!

You stumble and fall,
Look up,
Two bright eyes are looking with a piercing glare,
It's head darts like a coiled spring,
You feel a sharp nip at your ankle,
You have eight hours to live!

Stumbling through the jungle,
Five hours to live,
No hospital for miles.
Three hours to live,
The poison begins to have an effect.
Two hours to live,
Your eyelids droop.
You are another victim of the
Wanga Snake!

Max Crawford (10)
St Martin's Junior School, Epsom

10 Things I Hate About You

Number 1 you suck your thumb,
Number 2 I'm never with you,
Number 3 you can barely see,
Number 4 you always want more,
Number 5 you're always doing a dive
Number 6 you're always a mix,
Number 7 you're keen on heaven,
Number 8 you're always late,
Number 9 you're never fine, and
Number 10 you're always with certain men.

Shanel Shama (10)
St Martin's Junior School, Epsom

Too Many Cooks Spoil The Broth

My grandma said
He had a finger in every pie.
(He liked blueberry best.)

My auntie said
I was swinging the lead.
(It made my hands black.)

My mum tells me
Many hands make light work.
(I asked my friends if I could borrow theirs.)

My dad said
My brother had his head in the clouds.
(I wonder if it was cosy.)

My mum said
Every cloud has a silver lining.
(That must make them expensive.)

My friend said
Hold your horses.
(They pulled me away.)

Temi Oduyemi (9)
St Martin's Junior School, Epsom

The Zoo

I want to see the zoo, I said I want to see the zoo.
I want to see the lions roar and hear the parrots screech.
I want to see the monkeys fight and see the dolphins swim.
I want to see the zoo, I said I want to see the zoo.

I want to see the squirrels, I want to see them fly.
I want to see the rhino snort and see the elephant sneeze.
I want to see the snakes hiss and see them eat their prey.
I want to see the zoo, I said I want to see the zoo.

Emma Howlett (10)
St Martin's Junior School, Epsom

They Said

My brother said he had a finger in every pie.
(It was very hot.)

My mum said it was raining cats and dogs.
(I kept one as my pet.)

My sister said she'd lost her mind.
(I went off to look for it.)

My uncle said that I had got up on the wrong side of the bed.
(But I always got up on that side.)

The policeman said you have been caught red-handed.
(They still looked peach to me.)

My mum said you are a pain in the neck.
(I had one in my leg.)

My teacher said we could have a free hand.
(I tried to pull off my friend's.)

Ben Mawdsley (10)
St Martin's Junior School, Epsom

My Dog

I have a dog, his name is Sam
And this is what he eats:
Ham, frogs, mice and jam
And for a special treat.

I give him biscuits, milk and tea
And when he just wants a snack
He will gobble up an ant or bee
And when he's finished come galloping back.

I love him so very much,
And he loves me too,
So together we will clutch,
Through and through and through.

Farah Faheem (10)
St Martin's Junior School, Epsom

What Shall We Call It?

Honey, Buster, Rags or Tilly,
It's got to be sensible, not something silly.
Tom, Peter, Rabbit or Mitt,
What should we call it?

I'll ask my friends, you ask yours.
I can't wait to stroke its tiny paws.
We could teach it tricks and make it sit.
What should we call it?

It's coming tomorrow, I can't wait.
Bitsy, Mittsy, Muffin or Mate,
We still need a name for it.
What should we call it?

It's here today, it's so sweet.
Let's go and get it something to eat.
I'm glad we've got a name, the panic's over.
Here's the name, it's Rover!

Hannah Foxley (10)
St Martin's Junior School, Epsom

The Evacuees

Puffs of smoke stream out the train's funnel into the morning air,
I see them float into the sky on a journey to nowhere.
The doors open and what I see is truly of the worst,
Children standing helpless and weak like their hearts are fit to burst,
They all carry one suitcase in their trembling hand,
And look around to view their new homeland . . .

Andrew Taylor (10)
St Martin's Junior School, Epsom

My Best Friend

My best friend is rather kind
She helps me when I'm behind
She's true to her word and keeps a secret
We laugh and cheer all the time
She's there for me when I'm sad
She's really good not bad
If we have a break-up we're friends all day
We're always there for each other in each way
I've known her since the start of five
We were friends that day
She'll always be remembered by me
She's the best friend there could be
From all the fun times and the bad
I'll always remember her and be glad.

Joanna Faulkner (9)
St Martin's Junior School, Epsom

Myself

I am good at tennis
And I am a boy.
I find football fun
Which I play and enjoy.

I play lots of sport,
Lots of tennis.
My mum and dad say
I act like a menace.

I support Man United
Cheer for the goals.
Everyone tells me
I look like Paul Scholes.

Luke Tyrrell (10)
St Martin's Junior School, Epsom

My Mum Said . . .

My mum said I drive her round the bend,
(how could I? I don't have a driving licence!)

My dad said every cloud has a silver lining,
(I think that would make them heavy!)

My teacher said keep your hair on,
(it wasn't falling off!)

My friend said she would just be a minute,
(she was half an hour!)

My dinner lady said she had a finger in every pie,
(I could taste the finger bone!)

My sister said hold your horses,
(I don't have any!)

My brother said he was feeling under the weather,
(he wasn't, he was under our house roof!)

Isobel Barlow (9)
St Martin's Junior School, Epsom

I Don't Understand

My headteacher said this school cost an arm and a leg to build.
(I'm still trying to find the rest of the body.)

My mum tells me to put a sock in it.
(It didn't taste very nice.)

My auntie says every cloud has a silver lining.
(My dress has a silver lining.)

My uncle says many hands make light work.
(The only light I can see is the sun.)

My dad said he had a finger in every pie.
(I'm not sure if he has any fingers left.)

Emma Horrocks (10)
St Martin's Junior School, Epsom

My Noisy Sister

My sister is a chatterbox,
She goes on and on,
But still she is so noisy,
She doesn't seem to stop.

I lock her in the cupboard,
I shut her in a drawer,
I flush her down the toilet,
But still she goes on and on

I shut her in the bathroom,
I sit her on my bed,
I lock her in the freezer,
But still she is so noisy.

She just doesn't seem to stop, stop, stop!

Natasha Free (10)
St Martin's Junior School, Epsom

My Cousins

Daniel is like a trampoline,
Jamie's like a cake,
Ryan's like a football
And Amy likes to bake.

Hannah likes to play,
Kelly likes to teach,
Zoe likes to muck around
And Laura likes the beach.

Steven is like a mobile phone
And RJ is like an ice cream cone.

Rebecca Green (10)
St Martin's Junior School, Epsom

The Ghost

The ghost of the dead comes out at night
Giving people a scary fright
With a mighty roar he floats through the door
Fainting people with the sight.

The ghost of the dead comes out at night
Giving people a scary fright
With his ghostly friends he floats round the bend
The victim ran with all his might.

The ghost of the dead comes out at night
Giving people a scary fright
Later on he'll come again
After a kip in his den.

Hannah Veerapen (10)
St Martin's Junior School, Epsom

Little Sisters

They're as bouncy as beach balls,
As bright as the sun,
When they are around you know you'll have fun!

They're as sweet as sugar,
As funny as a clown,
One thing's for sure, you'll never feel down!

Sometimes they're annoying,
Sometimes they're a pain,
But they'll cheer you up, again and again!

Laura Cochrane (11)
St Martin's Junior School, Epsom

Time

One day when I went mad,
I had a great idea,
To travel back in time, I thought,
It was a great idea.

I made a time machine,
To take me back in time,
But something went wrong,
Luckily I'm fine.

There's one tiny problem,
I'm stuck back in time,
So I'm going to explore,
While I have the time.

I have to get back
To see my mum and dad,
If I don't get home,
Mum will go mad.

I'm now back home,
Wahoo! Yippee!
Let's just hope,
I'm back for tea.

Nicole Kelly (10)
St Martin's Junior School, Epsom

Winter

Woolly hats and jumpers out,
Lots of snow on the roundabout,
Christmas shopping in the crowds,
Children shouting really loud.

Icy ponds to skate on,
Put your socks and jumpers on,
No school for today,
So let's all go out and play!

Stephanie Edmonston (10)
St Martin's Junior School, Epsom

Once Upon A Dime

In the town of Nicotinell
Where the church bells rang like hell
To awaken the poor, deaden the old,
Marry the young and baptise the born

In the town of Nicotinell
Where the church bells rang like hell
Down in the ditches up on the hills
Where ever the wind lies still

In the town of Nicotinell
Where the church bells rang like hell
Climbing the trees, scouring the skies
Finding the gold where it lies

In the town of Nicotinell
Where the church bells rang like hell
With the dings and the dongs, the clangs and the
Clongs of the bells in the church

In the town of Nicotinell
Where the church bells rang like hell
Cutting off branches destroying nature
Stop it now it's getting later

In the town of Nicotinell
Where the church bells rang like hell
Make seed cake, brewing tea
As far as the eye can see.

Beatrice Glover (11)
St Martin's Junior School, Epsom

Mystery Valentine

I sent a card for a joke,
Not thinking that my friend
Had dreamed about a handsome bloke
And wished that he could be her Valentine.

She opened the card and looked inside,
It made her jump back in surprise,
The message there was all in rhyme,
And this is what it said:

You are my little superstar,
I often watch you from afar,
So I put this tribute together,
Just for you.

I love you like a red, red rose,
I love you when you wink and pose,
I love you when you pick your nose,
So be my Valentine.

If you're wondering who sent this to you
If you've really not a clue,
Then this is what you have to do.

Use your head and calculator,
Punch in 31773,
Once you've turned it upside-down,
I hope you won't be cross with me!

Ellie Broom (11)
St Martin's Junior School, Epsom

Rules In School

No running in the corridors,
No running up the stairs,
No sharing snacks at lunchtime,
No pulling people's hair,

No talking in assembly,
No talking in the class,
No chewing gum outside,
No playing balls near glass,

No answering back to your teacher,
No cheating in your tests,
No begging for some cash,
No being teachers' pests,

Rules, rules, rules
Who made them up?

Me!

Katie Sevenoaks (11)
St Martin's Junior School, Epsom

Thinking, Thoughts

It's midnight and I'm lying in my bed,
Thinking of all the things that I've said,
Yes, but no, but that's not fair!
I wanted that thing for my hair!

I listen to the rustling of the hedgehogs in the leaves,
And people robbing the shops, the little thieves,
I think of all the wrong things I've done in my life,
I sit up and then think twice.

Elizabeth Simmonds (11)
St Martin's Junior School, Epsom

Lost

A very respectable gentleman
Lost his wig the other day.
The wind was blowing very hard
And it was swept away!

He went to town
The very next day
And proclaimed,
'Find it for me and I will pay!'

A decent chap found the wig
Upon the head of a prize pig,
Gave it back, got the cash,
And kept in a secret stash.

The very respectable gentleman,
Lost his wig another day.
The wind was blowing very hard
And it was swept away!

Fiona Stamp (10)
St Martin's Junior School, Epsom

My Mum

As sweet as chocolate
Sleek as a snake
Fast as a cheetah
Hard as a rock
Loud as a whale
Gentle as velvet
Cuddly as a bear
Warm as a summer's day
Soft as silk
As fun as a dolphin
That's my generous Mum.

Rebecca Matthews (10)
St Martin's Junior School, Epsom

Aliens Have Landed!

There was an alien called Zog
Who looks like a big fat frog
He sits all day in his space bog
While drinking out of a log

We used to see him in the street
He had very big, smelly feet
And his clothes were never neat
And he never ate much meat

He has wet, slimy skin
And a strange double chin
He has committed many sins
And he has no loving kin

I have never seen him before
So I am not quite sure
What to do for I am poor
And I don't want to kick him out the door.

Nathan Saunders (10)
St Martin's Junior School, Epsom

I Took My Teddy To Nursery!

I took my teddy to nursery,
We went outside to play,
I took my teddy to nursery,
That was a terrible day.

I took my teddy to nursery,
I said he needed to be bathed,
I took my teddy to nursery,
My friends just stood there and laughed.

I took my teddy to nursery,
And there he will always stay,
I took my teddy to nursery,
For that terrible day.

Christopher Childs (11)
St Martin's Junior School, Epsom

Lessons

Lessons are like torture in a smelly old dungeon,
Lessons are more than I can bear.
Lessons, oh lessons, why do you haunt me?

Lessons, oh lessons, oh lessons, oh lessons
Are pointless in every way.
Lessons, oh lessons, oh lessons, oh lessons
Are a waste of a precious day!

Lessons are boring, it's plain, can't you see?
Teachers are like the heart of a lesson,
Why can't they back away?
Lessons, oh lessons, why do you haunt me?

Lessons, oh lessons, oh lessons, oh lessons
Are pointless in every way.
Lessons, oh lessons, oh lessons, oh lessons
Are a waste of a precious day.

Bethany Laws (9)
St Martin's Junior School, Epsom

I Was A Funky Chicken

I was a funky chicken
Who liked to eat his food.
I ate it all day long
Until I couldn't chew.

I was a funky chicken
Who liked to lay some eggs.
I sat up in the barnyard
Until I saw their heads.

I was a funky chicken
Who loved to go to sleep.
I found a bed in the graveyard
And unfortunately now I'm dead.

Josh Cuthbert (10)
St Martin's Junior School, Epsom

The Alien Saw The Computer

When the alien saw the computer,
He cried out, 'How absurd,
For the mouse doesn't squeak like a mouse,
Unlike on my home planet, Plurg.'

When the alien saw the computer,
He heard the speakers and cried,
'Where can this voice be coming from,
Is there a man inside?'

When the alien saw the computer,
He nearly got chickenpox,
He said, 'How is this a keyboard?
It can't open any locks!'

When the alien saw the computer,
He said, 'This is too weird for me,
I think I'll go back home,
Where I understand what I see.'

Jessica Walker (11)
St Martin's Junior School, Epsom

Big Brothers

I hate being the youngest,
I always get in trouble,
For getting in a muddle,
Brothers use me as an armrest.

My brothers always get in trouble,
But it's *me* who gets the blame,
My brothers always take my stuff,
And don't bring it back again.

My mum never listens to me,
And always listens to my brother,
I never get a rest from all this muddle,
Instead I just get in *trouble!*

Max Biddulph (11)
St Martin's Junior School, Epsom

I Have Got Lots Of Pets!

I have lots of pets.
People think I've got lots of pets.
They think that my cats are really silly
I've got a rat that sits in a hat.

I have lots of pets.
I've got lots of cats.
I've got a thin one
And one that eats too much.

I have lots of pets.
I've got lots of dogs.
I've got a big one
And one that looks like it's run into a wall.

I have lots of pets.
I've got lots of hamsters.
I've got a cute one
And a rough-looking one.

I have lots of pets.
I've got lots of fish.
I've got a very long one
And a blown up one.

William Clayton (10)
St Martin's Junior School, Epsom

The Day I Went Into Space

The day I went into space,
I looked like a big disgrace.
I hate the day I went to space.

I didn't even train,
And I got lots of fame.
For being the first man on Mars,
I hate the day I went to space.

I looked down below,
Saw the Earth glow.
I wish I was down there,
Eating a juicy pear.
I hate the day I went to space.

I can imagine aliens coming out of nowhere,
And blasting my brain under my hair.
I have to eat out of a solid tube,
It puts me in a very bad mood.
I hate the day I went to space.

Now you understand the point,
I hate the day I went to space!

Sonak Shah (11)
St Martin's Junior School, Epsom

London Wasps Vs Quins

Today's the big match,
Challenging my side.
The players all lead out,
Following my guide,

The match is starting.
I'd better be quick.
For I need to take my big kick,
5, 4, 3, 2, 1,

The whistle's gone.
I've taken my kick.
I was sin binned.
This drove me rather mad,

We were already three points ahead.
I was sent back on and I scored a wicked try.
The clapping in the background,
Made me rather proud.

In no time at all the match ended,
With the final score
Wasps 23 Quins 3.

Nicola Boult (11)
St Martin's Junior School, Epsom

Super Seasons

Winter is dreamy, a white wonderland.
Snowmen and snowballs, wind and rain,
Christmas and presents, family and friends.
Have a wonderful winter, I hope it never ends.

Super seasons, super seasons.

Autumn brings golden leaves,
Food and harvest, leaves and rain,
Coats and scarves, don't forget hats.
Have an enjoyable autumn with Hallowe'en bats.

Super seasons, super seasons.

Spring is super, a flower fantasy,
Bunnies and kittens, puppies and lambs,
Sun and rain.
Have an enjoyable spring and a daisy chain.

Super seasons, super seasons.

Summer is sunny, a red-hot day,
Trees and grass, sun and drought,
Water fights and hoses.
Have an enjoyable summer and some nice roses.

Danielle Carvey (10)
St Martin's Junior School, Epsom